KU-183-092

3 8003 00002 4083

BRAMPTON 10 MR

THE INTERNATIONAL
PSYCHO-ANALYTICAL
LIBRARY
No. 33

THE INTERNATIONAL PSYCHO-ANALYTICAL LIBRARY
EDITED BY M. MASUD R. KHAN
No. 33

SIGMUND FREUD

MOSES
AND MONOTHEISM
THREE ESSAYS

Translated and Edited
by
JAMES STRACHEY

LONDON
THE HOGARTH PRESS
AND THE INSTITUTE OF PSYCHO-ANALYSIS
1974

PUBLISHED BY
THE HOGARTH PRESS LTD
40 WILLIAM IV STREET
LONDON WC2N 4DG
*
CLARKE, IRWIN AND CO LTD
TORONTO

All rights reserved. No part of this publication may be reproduced, stored in a retrieval system, or transmitted in any form, or by any means, electronic, mechanical, photocopying, recording or otherwise, without the prior permission of The Hogarth Press Ltd.

This Translation First Published 1964
This Corrected Edition First Published 1974

ISBN 0 7012 0120 7

TRANSLATION AND EDITORIAL MATTER
© ANGELA RICHARDS AND THE INSTITUTE
OF PSYCHO-ANALYSIS 1964

PRINTED IN GREAT BRITAIN BY
REDWOOD BURN LIMITED
TROWBRIDGE AND ESHER

EDITORIAL NOTE

Since the original publication of the English translations of Freud's works there has appeared the new authoritative text of *The Standard Edition of the Complete Psychological Works of Sigmund Freud*, translated from the German under the general editorship of James Strachey, in collaboration with Anna Freud, assisted by Alix Strachey, Alan Tyson and Angela Richards. The Institute of Psycho-Analysis therefore thought it would be desirable to use this new text when reprinting the International Psycho-Analytical Library edition as the stocks of these began to get low. With the generous co-operation of the late Mr. Strachey and his collaborators, this aim has been achieved, and now as it becomes necessary to reprint any of Freud's works they are appearing in new editions in the International Psycho-Analytical Library with the text of *The Standard Edition.*

The present edition of Freud's *Moses and Monotheism* contains the completely revised and fully annotated text of *The Standard Edition*. A bibliography and index have been provided.

It is the hope of the Publications Committee that these revised texts with their annotations will be useful to the growing number of students and readers of psycho-analysis.

M. Masud R. Khan
Editor
The International Psycho-Analytical Library

CONTENTS

EDITOR'S NOTE

DER MANN MOSES UND DIE MONOTHEISTISCHE RELIGION: DREI ABHANDLUNGEN

(*a*) German Editions:

1939 Amsterdam: Verlag Allert de Lange. Pp. 241.

1950 *G.W.*, **16,** 101–246.

(*b*) English Translation:

Moses and Monotheism

1939 London: Hogarth Press and Institute of Psycho-Analysis. Pp. 223. New York: Knopf. Pp. viii + 218. (Tr. Katherine Jones.)

1964 *S.E.*, **22**, 1–137. (Tr. James Strachey.)

The present translation is a corrected reprint of the *Standard Edition* version, with a few editorial additions.

The first two of the three essays that make up this work appeared originally in 1937 in *Imago*, **23** (1), 5–13 and (4), 387–419; English translations of these two appeared in *Int. J. Psycho-Anal.*, **19** (3) (1938), 291–8, and **20** (1) (1939), 1–32. Section C of Part II of the third essay was read on the author's behalf by Anna Freud at the Paris International Psycho-Analytical Congress on August 2, 1938, and was afterwards published separately in *Int. Z. Psychoanal. Imago*, **24** (1/2) (1939), 6–9, under the title 'Der Fortschritt in der Geistigkeit' ('The Advance in Intellectuality'). The first essay and the first three sections of the second essay were included in *Almanach 1938*, 9–43. Only a very few unimportant changes were made in these earlier publications when they were included in the complete work. These changes are noted in the present edition.

It was apparently during the summer of 1934 that Freud completed his first draft of this book, with the title: *The Man Moses, a Historical Novel* (Jones, 1957, 206). In a long letter to Arnold Zweig of September 30, 1934 (included in Freud, 1960*a*, and 1968*a*), he gave an account of the book, as well as of his reasons for not publishing it. These were much the same as those which he explains in the first of his prefatory notes to the third essay below (p. 54)—namely, on the one hand, doubts as to whether his argument was sufficiently well established and, on the other hand, fears of the reactions to its publication by the Roman Catholic hierarchy who were at that time dominant in the Austrian government. From the account which he then gave of the work itself, it sounds essentially the same as what we now have—even its form, in three separate sections, has remained unchanged. Nevertheless, changes must have been made in it. Freud was constantly expressing his dissatisfaction with it—in particular with the third essay. There appears to have been a general re-writing during the summer of 1936, though what we are told on the subject is far from clear (Jones, 1957, 388). At all events, the first essay was published at the beginning of the following year (1937) and the second at its end.[1] But the third essay was still held back and only finally passed for printing after Freud's arrival in England in the spring of 1938. The book was printed that autumn in Holland and the English translation was published in the following March.

What is perhaps likely to strike a reader first about *Moses and Monotheism* is a certain unorthodoxy, or even eccentricity, in its construction: three essays of greatly differing length, two prefaces, both situated at the beginning of the third essay, and a third preface situated half-way through that same essay, constant recapitulations and repetitions—such irregularities are unknown elsewhere in Freud's writings, and he himself points them out and apologizes for them more than once. Their explanation? Undoubtedly the circumstances of the book's composition: the long period—four years or more—during which it was being constantly revised, and the acute external difficulties of the final phase, with a succession of political disorders in Austria culminating in the Nazi occupation of Vienna and Freud's enforced migration to England. That the outcome of these influences was to be seen only in the restricted and temporary field of this single volume is very conclusively proved by the work which immediately followed this one—the *Outline*

[1] The latter was finished on August 11, 1937 (Letter to Marie Bonaparte, dated August 13, 1937, No. 290 in Freud, 1960*a*).

of Psycho-Analysis, among the most concise and well-organized of Freud's writings.

But if *Moses and Monotheism* is judged to lack something in its form of presentation, that is not to imply a criticism of the interest of its content or of the cogency of its arguments. Its historical basis is no doubt a matter for expert dispute, but the ingenuity with which the psychological developments fit in with the premisses is likely to persuade the reader who is without prepossession. Those, in particular, who are familiar with the psycho-analysis of the individual will be fascinated to see the same succession of developments exhibited in an analysis of a national group. The whole work is, of course, to be regarded as a continuation of Freud's earlier studies of the origins of human social organization in *Totem and Taboo* (1912–13) and *Group Psychology* (1921*c*). A very elaborate and informative discussion of the book will be found in Chapter XIII of the third volume of Ernest Jones's biography (1957), 388–401.

Editorial additions, whether to the text or the footnotes, are printed in square brackets.

A NOTE ON THE TRANSCRIPTION OF PROPER NAMES

THE occurrence in *Moses and Monotheism* of a large number of Egyptian and Hebrew names presents the translator with some special problems.

Egyptian writing does not in general record the vowels, so that the actual pronunciation of Egyptian names can only be guessed by a hazardous process of inferences. Various conventional renderings have therefore been adopted by various authorities. For instance, in discussing this question, Gardiner (1927, Appendix B) quotes four different versions of the name of the owner of a well-known tomb at Thebes: Tehutihetep, Thuthotep, Thothotpou and Dhuthotpe. Just as many varieties are to be found of the name of the 'heretic king', who figures so prominently here in Freud's argument. The choice seems to be governed a good deal by nationality. Thus, in the past, English Egyptologists were inclined to Akhnaton, the Germans preferred Echnaton, the American (Breasted) chose Ikhnaton, and the great Frenchman (Maspero) decided for Khouniatonou. Faced by these alluring alternatives, the present translator has fallen back on the humdrum version which has for many years been adopted by the *Journal of Egyptian Archaeology* and seems now to be the one becoming most generally accepted, at least in English-speaking countries: Akhenaten.[1] This same authority has been generally followed in the transcription of all other Egyptian names.

As regards Old Testament names, the answer has been simpler, and the forms found in the English Authorized Version have been employed. It must be added, however, that the unmentionable name of the Deity is here given the transcription regularly found in the works of English scholars: Yahweh.

[1] See, for example, Lindon Smith, *Tombs, Temples and Ancient Art*, University of Oklahoma Press, 1956, and *The Times*, April 2, 1963, p. 14, column 5. Different versions of the name will necessarily be found where Freud quotes from other writers.

I

MOSES AN EGYPTIAN

To deprive a people of the man whom they take pride in as the greatest of their sons is not a thing to be gladly or carelessly undertaken, least of all by someone who is himself one of them. But we cannot allow any such reflection to induce us to put the truth aside in favour of what are supposed to be national interests; and, moreover, the clarification of a set of facts may be expected to bring us a gain in knowledge.

The man Moses,[1] who set the Jewish people free, who gave them their laws and founded their religion, dates from such remote times that we cannot evade a preliminary enquiry as to whether he was a historical personage or a creature of legend. If he lived, it was in the thirteenth, though it may have been in the fourteenth, century before Christ. We have no information about him except from the sacred books of the Jews and their traditions as recorded in writing. Although a decision on the question thus lacks final certainty, an overwhelming majority of historians have nevertheless pronounced in favour of the view that Moses was a real person and that the Exodus from Egypt associated with him did in fact take place. It is justly argued that the later history of the people of Israel would be incomprehensible if this premiss were not accepted. Indeed, science to-day has become altogether more circumspect and handles traditions far more indulgently than in the early days of historical criticism.

The first thing that attracts our attention about the figure of Moses is his name, which is 'Mosheh' in Hebrew. 'What is its origin?' we may ask, 'and what does it mean?' As we know, the account in the second chapter of *Exodus* already provides an answer. We are told there that the Egyptian princess who rescued the infant boy from exposure in the Nile gave him that name, putting forward an etymological reason: 'because I drew

[1] [Moses is so spoken of in the Bible (cf. *Numbers*, xii, 3), and the phrase occurs repeatedly in this work. It will be recalled that the title of the German original is, literally, *The Man Moses and Monotheist Religion.*]

him out of the water'.[1] This explanation, however, is clearly inadequate. 'The Biblical interpretation of the name as "he who was drawn out of the water" ', argues a writer in the *Jüdisches Lexikon*,[2] 'is popular etymology, with which, to begin with, it is impossible to harmonize the *active* form of the Hebrew word—for "*Mosheh*" can at most only mean "he who draws out".' We can support this rejection by two further arguments: in the first place, it is absurd to attribute to an Egyptian princess a derivation of the name from the Hebrew, and secondly, the water out of which the child was drawn was most probably not the water of the Nile.

On the other hand, a suspicion has long been expressed, and in many different quarters, that the name 'Moses' is derived from the Egyptian vocabulary. Instead of enumerating all the authorities who have argued in this sense, I will quote the relevant passage from a comparatively recent book, *The Dawn of Conscience* (1934), by J. H. Breasted, a writer whose *History of Egypt* (1906) is regarded as a standard work: 'It is important to notice that his name, Moses, was Egyptian. It is simply the Egyptian word "mose" meaning "child", and is an abridgement of a fuller form of such names as "Amen-mose" meaning "Amon-a-child" or "Ptah-mose" meaning "Ptah-a-child", these forms themselves being likewise abbreviations for the complete form "Amon-(has-given)-a-child" or "Ptah-(has-given)-a-child". The abbreviation "child" early became a convenient rapid form for the cumbrous full name, and the name Mose, "child", is not uncommon on the Egyptian monuments. The father of Moses without doubt prefixed to his son's name that of an Egyptian god like Amon or Ptah, and this divine name was gradually lost in current usage, till the boy was called "Mose". (The final *s* is an addition drawn from the Greek translation of the Old Testament. It is not in the Hebrew which has "Mosheh").' [3] I have repeated this passage word for word and I am by no means ready to share responsibility for its details. I am also rather surprised that Breasted has failed to mention precisely the analogous theophorous

[1] [*Exodus*, ii, 10.—In this translation, all quotations from the Scriptures are given in the Authorized Version.]

[2] Herlitz and Kirschner (1930), **4** [(1), 303]. [The contributor quoted was M. Soloweitschik.]

[3] Breasted, 1934, 350.

names which figure in the list of Egyptian kings, such as Ahmose, Thoth-mose and Ra-mose.

Now we should have expected that one of the many people who have recognized that 'Moses' is an Egyptian name would also have drawn the conclusion or would at least have considered the possibility that the person who bore this Egyptian name may himself have been an Egyptian. In relation to modern times we have no hesitation in drawing such conclusions, though nowadays people bear not one name but two —a family name and a personal name—and though a change of name or the adoption of a similar one in fresh circumstances is not beyond possibility. Thus we are not in the least surprised to find it confirmed that the poet Chamisso[1] was French by birth, that Napoleon Buonaparte, on the other hand, was of Italian extraction and that Benjamin Disraeli was indeed an Italian Jew, as we should expect from his name. In relation to ancient and primitive times, one would have thought that a conclusion such as this as to a person's nationality based on his name would have seemed far more reliable and in fact unimpeachable. Nevertheless, so far as I know, no historian has drawn this conclusion in the case of Moses—not even any of those who, once again like Breasted himself (1934, 354), are ready to assume that 'Moses was learned in all the wisdom of the Egyptians'.[2]

What prevented their doing so cannot be judged with certainty. Possibly their reverence for Biblical tradition was invincible. Possibly the notion that the man Moses might have been anything but a Hebrew seemed too monstrous. However that may be, it emerges that the recognition that the name of Moses is Egyptian has not been looked upon as affording decisive evidence of his origin, and that no further conclusions

[1] [Adelbert von Chamisso (1781–1838) author of *Frauenliebe und -leben*, a cycle of lyrics set to music by Schumann, and *Peter Schlemihl*, the story of the man who sold his shadow.]

[2] Although the suspicion that Moses was an Egyptian has been voiced often enough without reference to his name, from the earliest times up to the present. [Freud had quoted a comic anecdote to that effect in his *Introductory Lectures* (1916–17), *Standard Ed.*, **15**, 161.—This footnote appeared first in the 1939 edition. It is not included in the original *Imago* version of 1937 or in the English translation of 1939.—The phrase quoted from Breasted is in fact derived from a speech by St. Stephen (*Acts*, vii, 22).]

have been drawn from it. If the question of this great man's nationality is regarded as important, it would seem to be desirable to bring forward fresh material that would help towards answering it.

That is what my short paper aims at doing. Its claim to be given a place in the pages of *Imago* rests on the fact that the substance of what it has to contribute is an application of psycho-analysis. The argument arrived at in this way will undoubtedly only impress that minority of readers who are familiar with analytic thinking and who are able to appreciate its findings. To them, however, it will, I hope, appear significant.

In 1909 Otto Rank, who was at that time still under my influence, published, following a suggestion of mine, a book bearing the title *Der Mythus von der Geburt des Helden.*[1] It deals with the fact that 'almost all the prominent civilized nations . . . began at an early stage to glorify their heroes, legendary kings and princes, founders of religions, dynasties, empires or cities, in brief their national heroes, in a number of poetic tales and legends. The history of the birth and of the early life of these personalities came to be especially invested with phantastic features, which, in different peoples, even though widely separated by space and entirely independent of each other, present a baffling similarity and in part, indeed, a literal conformity. Many investigators have been impressed with this fact, which has long been recognized.' [P.1.] If, following Rank, we construct (by a technique a little like Galton's[2]) an 'average legend' that brings into prominence the essential features of all these stories, we arrive at the following picture:

'The hero is the child of the *most aristocratic* parents; usually the son of a king.

'His conception is preceded by difficulties, such as abstinence or prolonged barrenness or his parents having to have

[1] [*The Myth of the Birth of the Hero.*] It is far from being my intention to belittle the value of Rank's independent contributions to the work. [The quotations which follow are based on the translation by Robbins and Jelliffe, first published in 1914, to which the page references in the text also relate. Some changes have been made in the interests of greater accuracy.]

[2] [Freud has in mind Galton's 'composite photographs' to which he was fond of referring. See, for instance, *The Interpretation of Dreams* (1900*a*), *Standard Ed.*, **4**, 139.]

intercourse in secret owing to external prohibitions or obstacles. During the pregnancy, or even earlier, there is a prophecy (in the form of a dream or oracle) cautioning against his birth, usually threatening danger to his father.

'As a result of this the new-born child is condemned to death or to *exposure*, usually by the orders of *his father or of someone representing him*; as a rule he is given over to the *water* in a *casket*.

'He is afterwards *rescued* by animals or by *humble people* (such as *shepherds*) and is suckled by a *female animal* or by a *humble woman*.

'After he has grown up, he rediscovers his aristocratic parents after highly variegated experiences, *takes his revenge on his father*, on the one hand, and is *acknowledged* on the other and achieves greatness and fame.' [P. 61.]

The oldest of the historical figures to whom this myth of birth is attached is Sargon of Agade, the founder of Babylon (*c.* 2800 B.C.). For us in particular it will not be without interest to quote the account of it, which is attributed to him himself:

'Sargon, the mighty King, the King of Agade am I. *My mother was a Vestal, my father I knew not*, while my father's brother dwelt in the mountains. In my city, Azupirani, which lies on the bank of the Euphrates, my mother, the Vestal, conceived me. *Secretly she bore me. She laid me in a coffer made of reeds*, closed my doorway with pitch, and *let me down into the river*, which did not drown me. The river carried me to Akki, the drawer of water. Akki, the drawer of water, lifted me out in the kindness of his heart. *Akki, the drawer of water, brought me up as his own son.* Akki, the drawer of water, made me his gardener. While I worked as a gardener, [the goddess] Ishtar grew fond of me, I became King and for forty-five years I held kingly sway.' [Pp. 12–13.]

The names most familiar to us in the series which begins with Sargon of Agade are Moses, Cyrus and Romulus. But in addition to these Rank has brought together a whole number of other heroic figures from poetry or legend, of whom the same story of their youth is told, either in its entirety or in easily recognizable fragments—including Oedipus, Karna, Paris, Telephos, Perseus, Heracles, Gilgamesh, Amphion and Zethos, and others.[1]

[1] [Karna was a hero in the Sanskrit epic *Mahabharata*, Gilgamesh was a Babylonian hero and the remainder were figures in Greek mythology.]

Rank's researches have made us acquainted with the source and purpose of this myth. I need only refer to them with some brief indications. A hero is someone who has had the courage to rebel against his father and has in the end victoriously overcome him. Our myth traces this struggle back as far as the individual's prehistory, for it represents him as being born against his father's will and rescued despite his father's evil intention. The exposure in a casket is an unmistakable symbolic representation of birth: the casket is the womb and the water is the amniotic fluid. The parent-child relationship is represented in countless dreams by pulling out of the water or rescuing from the water.[1] When a people's imagination attaches the myth of birth which we are discussing to an outstanding figure, it is intending in that way to recognize him as a hero and to announce that he has fulfilled the regular pattern of a hero's life. In fact, however, the source of the whole poetic fiction is what is known as a child's 'family romance', in which the son reacts to a change in his emotional relation to his parents and in particular to his father.[2] A child's earliest years are dominated by an enormous overvaluation of his father; in accordance with this a king and queen in dreams and fairy tales invariably stand for parents. Later, under the influence of rivalry and of disappointment in real life, the child begins to detach himself from his parents and to adopt a critical attitude towards his father. Thus the two families in the myth—the aristocratic one and the humble one—are both of them reflections of the child's own family as they appeared to him in successive periods of his life.

We may fairly say that these explanations make the widespread and uniform nature of myths of the birth of heroes fully intelligible. For that reason it is all the more deserving of interest that the legend of the birth and exposure of Moses occupies a special position and, indeed, in one essential respect contradicts the rest.

Let us start from the two families between which, according to the legend, the child's destiny is played out. According to the

[1] [See, for instance, *The Interpretation of Dreams* (1900*a*), *Standard Ed.*, **5**, 399–402 and 404.]

[2] [Cf. Freud's paper 'Family Romances' (1909*c*). That paper was first published as a part of the volume by Rank which has been quoted above.]

analytic interpretation, as we know, the families are one and the same and are only differentiated chronologically. In the typical form of the legend, it is the first family, the one into which the child is born, which is the aristocratic one, most often of royal rank; the second family, the one in which the child grows up, is the one that is humble or has fallen on evil days. This tallies, moreover, with the circumstances [of the 'family romance'] to which the interpretation traces the legend back. Only in the legend of Oedipus is this difference blurred: the child which has been exposed by one royal family is received by another royal couple. It can scarcely be by chance, one feels, that precisely in this example the original identity of the two families may be dimly perceived in the legend itself. The social contrast between the two families provides the myth—which, as we know, is designed to stress the heroic nature of a great man—with a second function which becomes of special significance when applied to historical personages. For the myth can also be employed to create a patent of nobility for the hero, to raise his social standing. To the Medes, Cyrus was a foreign conqueror; but by means of a legend of exposure he became the grandson of their king. The same applies to Romulus. If any such person existed, he must have been an adventurer of unknown origin, an upstart; the legend, however, made him offspring and heir of the royal house of Alba Longa.

With Moses things were quite different. In his case the first family, elsewhere the aristocratic one, was sufficiently modest. He was the child of Jewish Levites. But the place of the second family, elsewhere the humble one, was taken by the royal house of Egypt; the princess brought him up as her own son. This deviation from type has puzzled many people. Eduard Meyer,[1] and others following him, assumed that originally the legend was different. Pharaoh, according to them, had been warned by a prophetic dream[2] that a son born to his daughter would bring danger to him and his kingdom. He therefore had the child exposed in the Nile after his birth. But he was rescued by Jewish people and brought up as their child. For 'nationalist motives' (as Rank puts it[3]) the legend would then have been given the modified form in which we know it.

[1] [Meyer, 1906, 46 f.]

[2] This is also mentioned in the account given by Flavius Josephus.

[3] Rank, 1909, 80 *n.*

A moment's reflection, however, tells us that an original legend of Moses like this, one no longer deviating from the other legends, cannot have existed. For it was either of Egyptian or of Jewish origin. The first alternative is ruled out: the Egyptians had no motive for glorifying Moses, since he was no hero to them. We are to suppose, then, that the legend was created among the Jewish people—that is to say, that it was attached in its familiar form [i.e. in the typical form of a birth-legend] to the figure of their leader. But it was totally unsuitable for that purpose, for what would be the use to a people of a legend which made their great man into a foreigner?

The legend of Moses, in the form in which we have it to-day, falls notably short of its secret intention. If Moses was not of royal birth, the legend could not stamp him as a hero; if it left him as a Jewish child, it had done nothing to raise his social standing. Only one small fragment of the entire myth remains effective: the assurance that the child had survived in the face of powerful external forces. (This feature recurs in the story of the childhood of Jesus, in which King Herod takes over the role of Pharaoh.) Thus we are in fact free to suppose that some later and clumsy adapter of the material of the legend found an opportunity for introducing into the story of his hero Moses something which resembled the classical exposure legends marking out a hero, but which, on account of the special circumstances of the case, was not applicable to Moses.

Our investigations might have had to rest content with this inconclusive and, moreover, uncertain outcome, and they might have done nothing towards answering the question of whether Moses was an Egyptian. There is, however, another and perhaps more hopeful line of approach to an assessment of the legend of exposure.

Let us return to the two families of the myth. At the level of analytic interpretation they are, as we know, identical; whereas at the level of the myth they are differentiated into an aristocratic family and a humble one. Where, however, the figure to whom the myth is attached is a historical one, there is a third level—that of reality. One of the families is the real one, in which the person in question (the great man) was actually born and grew up; the other is fictitious, fabricated by the myth in pursuit of its own intentions. As a rule the humble family is the real one and the aristocratic family the fabricated one. The situation in the case of Moses seemed somehow different. And here the new line of approach will perhaps lead to a clarification: in every instance which it has been possible to test, the first family, the one from which the child was exposed, was the invented one, and the second one, in which he was received and grew up, was the real one. If we have the courage to recognize this assertion as universally true and as applying also to the legend of Moses, then all at once we see things clearly: Moses was an Egyptian—probably an aristocrat—whom the legend was designed to turn into a Jew. And that would be our conclusion. The exposure in the water was at its correct point in the story; but, in order to fit in with the fresh purpose, its aim had to be somewhat violently twisted. From being a way of sacrificing the child, it was turned into a means of rescuing him.

The deviation of the legend of Moses from all the others of its kind can be traced back to a special feature of his history. Whereas normally a hero, in the course of his life, rises above his humble beginnings, the heroic life of the man Moses began with his stepping down from his exalted position and descending to the level of the Children of Israel.

We started on this brief enquiry in the expectation of deriving a fresh argument from it in support of the suspicion that Moses was an Egyptian. We have seen that the first argument, based on his name, failed with many people to carry conviction.[1] We must be prepared to find that this new argument, based on an analysis of the legend of exposure, may have no better success. It will no doubt be objected that the circumstances of the

[1] Thus Eduard Meyer writes (1905, 651): 'The name "Moses" is probably Egyptian, and the name "Pinchas" in the priestly family of Shiloh . . . is undoubtedly Egyptian. Of course this does not prove that these families were of Egyptian origin, but, no doubt, that they had connections with Egypt.' We may ask, to be sure, what sort of connections this is supposed to make us think of. [This paper by Meyer (1905) is a *résumé* of a very much longer one (1906) where the question of these Egyptian names is further examined (450–1). From this it appears that there were two men called 'Pinchas' ('Phinehas' in the Authorized Version)—one a grandson of Aaron (*Exodus*, vi, 25 and *Numbers*, xxv, 7) and the other a priest at Shiloh (I *Samuel*, i, 3), both of them Levites. (Cf. p. 39 below.) Shiloh was the place where the Ark was stationed before its ultimate removal to Jerusalem. (Cf. *Joshua*, xviii, 1.)]

construction and transformation of legends are, after all, too obscure to justify a conclusion such as ours and that the traditions surrounding the heroic figure of Moses—with all their confusion and contradictions and their unmistakable signs of centuries of continuous and tendentious revisions and superimpositions—are bound to baffle every effort to bring to light the kernel of historical truth that lies behind them. I do not myself share this dissenting attitude but neither am I in a position to refute it.

If no more certainty could be reached than this, why, it may be asked, have I brought this enquiry into public notice at all? I am sorry to say that even my justification for doing so cannot go beyond hints. For if one allows oneself to be carried away by the two arguments which I have put forward here, and if one sets out to take the hypothesis seriously that Moses was an aristocratic Egyptian, very interesting and far-reaching prospects are opened up. With the help of some not very remote assumptions, we shall, I believe, be able to understand the motives which led Moses in the unusual step he took and, closely related to this, to obtain a grasp of the possible basis of a number of the characteristics and peculiarities of the laws and religion which he gave to the Jewish people; and we shall even be led on to important considerations regarding the origin of monotheist religions in general. Such weighty conclusions cannot, however, be founded on psychological probabilities alone. Even if one accepts the fact of Moses being an Egyptian as a first historical foothold, one would need to have at least a second firm fact in order to defend the wealth of emerging possibilities against the criticism of their being a product of the imagination and too remote from reality. Objective evidence of the period to which the life of Moses and with it the Exodus from Egypt are to be referred would perhaps have fulfilled this requirement. But this has not been obtainable, and it will therefore be better to leave unmentioned any further implications of the discovery that Moses was an Egyptian.

II

IF MOSES WAS AN EGYPTIAN . . .

In an earlier contribution to this periodical,[1] I attempted to bring up a fresh argument in support of the hypothesis that the man Moses, the liberator and law-giver of the Jewish people, was not a Jew but an Egyptian. It had long been observed that his name was derived from the Egyptian vocabulary, though the fact had not been properly appreciated. What I added was that the interpretation of the myth of exposure which was linked with Moses necessarily led to the inference that he was an Egyptian whom the needs of a people sought to make into a Jew. I remarked at the end of my paper that important and far-reaching implications followed from the hypothesis that Moses was an Egyptian, but that I was not prepared to argue publicly in favour of these implications, since they were based only on psychological probabilities and lacked any objective proof. The greater the importance of the views arrived at in this way, the more strongly one feels the need to beware of exposing them without a secure basis to the critical assaults of the world around one—like a bronze statue with feet of clay. Not even the most tempting probability is a protection against error; even if all the parts of a problem seem to fit together like the pieces of a jig-saw puzzle, one must reflect that what is probable is not necessarily the truth and that the truth is not always probable. And lastly, it did not seem attractive to find oneself classed with the schoolmen and Talmudists who delight in exhibiting their ingenuity without regard to how remote from reality their thesis may be.

Notwithstanding these hesitations, which weigh as much with me to-day as they did before, the outcome of my conflicting motives is a decision to produce the present sequel to my earlier communication. But once again this is not the whole story nor the most important part of the whole story.

[1] *Imago*, **23** (1937). [Essay I above.]

(1)

If, then, Moses was an Egyptian—our first yield from this hypothesis is a fresh enigma and one which it is hard to solve. If a people or a tribe[1] sets out upon a great undertaking, it is only to be expected that one of its members will take his place as their leader or will be chosen for that post. But it is not easy to guess what could induce an aristocratic Egyptian—a prince, perhaps, or a priest or high official—to put himself at the head of a crowd of immigrant foreigners at a backward level of civilization and to leave his country with them. The well-known contempt felt by the Egyptians for foreign nationals makes such a proceeding particularly unlikely. Indeed I could well believe that this has been precisely why even those historians who have recognized that the man's name was Egyptian, and who have ascribed to him all the wisdom of the Egyptians [p. 9], have been unwilling to accept the obvious possibility that Moses was an Egyptian.

This first difficulty is promptly followed by another. We must not forget that Moses was not only the political leader of the Jews settled in Egypt but was also their law-giver and educator and forced them into the service of a new religion, which to this very day is known after him as the Mosaic one. But is it so easy for one single man to create a new religion? And if anyone wishes to influence another person's religion, would he not most naturally convert him to his own? The Jewish people in Egypt were certainly not without a religion of some form or other; and if Moses, who gave them a new one, was an Egyptian, the presumption cannot be put aside that this other new religion was the Egyptian one.

There is something that stands in the way of this possibility: the fact of there being the most violent contrast between the Jewish religion which is attributed to Moses and the religion of Egypt. The former is a rigid monotheism on the grand scale: there is only one God, he is the sole God, omnipotent, unapproachable; his aspect is more than human eyes can tolerate, no image must be made of him, even his name may not be spoken. In the Egyptian religion there is an almost innumerable host of deities of varying dignity and origin: a few personifica-

[1] We have no notion of what numbers were concerned in the Exodus from Egypt.

tions of great natural forces such as heaven and earth, sun and moon, an occasional abstraction such as Ma'at (truth or justice) or a caricature such as the dwarf-like Bes; but most of them local gods, dating from the period when the country was divided into numerous provinces, with the shape of animals, as though they had not yet completed their evolution from the old totem animals, with no sharp distinctions between them, and scarcely differing in the functions allotted to them. The hymns in honour of these gods say almost the same things about all of them, and identify them with one another unhesitatingly, in a manner hopelessly confusing to us. The names of gods are combined with one another, so that one of them may almost be reduced to being an epithet of the other. Thus, in the heyday of the 'New Kingdom' the principal god of the city of Thebes was called Amen-Re'; the first part of this compound stands for the ram-headed god of the city, while Re' is the name of the falcon-headed sun-god of On [Heliopolis]. Magical and ceremonial acts, charms and amulets dominated the service of these gods as they did the daily life of the Egyptians.

Some of these differences may easily be derived from the fundamental contrast between a strict monotheism and an unrestricted polytheism. Others are evidently the result of a difference in spiritual and intellectual[1] level, since one of these religions is very close to primitive phases [of development], while the other has risen to the heights of sublime abstraction. It may be due to these two factors that one occasionally has an impression that the contrast between the Mosaic and the Egyptian religions is a deliberate one and has been intentionally heightened—when, for instance, one of them condemns magic and sorcery in the severest terms, while in the other they proliferate with the greatest luxuriance, or when the insatiable appetite of the Egyptians for embodying their gods in clay, stone and metal (to which our museums owe so much to-day) is confronted with the harsh prohibition against making an image of any living or imagined creature.

But there is still another contrast between the two religions which is not met by the explanations we have attempted. No other people of antiquity did so much [as the Egyptians] to

[1] ['*Geistig*' is the word here translated 'spiritual and intellectual'. This concept becomes of great importance towards the end of this work, especially in Section C of Part II of Essay III. Cf. the footnote on p. 86.]

deny death or took such pains to make existence in the next world possible. And accordingly Osiris, the god of the dead, the ruler of this other world, was the most popular and undisputed of all the gods of Egypt. On the other hand the ancient Jewish religion renounced immortality entirely; the possibility of existence continuing after death is nowhere and never mentioned. And this is all the more remarkable since later experiences have shown that belief in an after-life is perfectly well compatible with a monotheist religion.

It was our hope that the hypothesis that Moses was an Egyptian would turn out to be fruitful and illuminating in various directions. But the first conclusion we drew from that hypothesis—that the new religion which he gave to the Jews was his own Egyptian one—has been invalidated by our realization of the different, and indeed contradictory, character of the two religions.

(2)

Another possibility is opened to us by a remarkable event in the history of the Egyptian religion, an event which has only lately been recognized and appreciated. It remains possible that the religion which Moses gave to his Jewish people was nevertheless his own—that it was *an* Egyptian religion, though not *the* Egyptian religion.

In the glorious Eighteenth Dynasty, under which Egypt first became a world power, a young Pharaoh came to the throne in about the year 1375 B.C. To begin with he was called, like his father, Amenophis (IV), but later he changed his name and not only his name. This king set about forcing a new religion on his Egyptian subjects—a religion which ran contrary to their thousands-of-years-old traditions and to all the familiar habits of their lives. It was a strict monotheism, the first attempt of the kind, so far as we know, in the history of the world, and along with the belief in a single god religious intolerance was inevitably born, which had previously been alien to the ancient world and remained so long afterwards. The reign of Amenophis, however, lasted for only seventeen years. Very soon after his death in 1358 B.C., the new religion was swept away and the memory of the heretic king was proscribed. What little we know of him is derived from the ruins of the new royal capital which he built and dedicated to his god and from the inscriptions in the rock tombs adjacent to it. Whatever we can learn about this remarkable and, indeed, unique personality is deserving of the highest interest.[1]

Every novelty must have its preliminaries and preconditions in something earlier. The origins of Egyptian monotheism can be traced back a little way with some certainty.[2] For a considerable time, tendencies had been at work among the priesthood of the sun temple at On (Heliopolis) in the direction of developing the idea of a universal god and of emphasizing the ethical side of his nature. Ma'at, the goddess of truth, order and justice, was a daughter of the sun god Re'. During the reign of Amenophis III, the father and predecessor of the reformer, the worship of the sun god had already gained a new impetus—probably in opposition to Amun of Thebes, who had become too powerful. A very ancient name of the sun god, Aten or Atum, was brought into fresh prominence, and the young king found in this Aten religion a movement ready to hand, which he did not have to be the first to inspire but of which he could become an adherent.

The political conditions in Egypt had begun at this time to exercise a lasting influence on the Egyptian religion. As a result of the military exploits of the great conqueror, Tuthmosis III, Egypt had become a world power: the empire now included Nubia in the south, Palestine, Syria and a part of Mesopotamia in the north. This imperialism was reflected in religion as universalism and monotheism. Since the Pharaoh's responsibilities now embraced not only Egypt but Nubia and Syria as well, deity too was obliged to abandon its national limitation and, just as the Pharaoh was the sole and unrestricted ruler of the world known to the Egyptians, this must also apply to the Egyptians' new deity. Moreover, with the extension of the empire's frontiers, it was natural that Egypt would become more accessible to foreign influences; some of the royal wives were Asiatic princesses,[3] and it is possible that direct

[1] Breasted [1906, 356] calls him 'the first individual in human history'.

[2] What follows is in the main based on the accounts given by Breasted (1906 and 1934) and in the relevant sections of the *Cambridge Ancient History*, Vol. II [1924].

[3] This may perhaps be true even of Nefertiti, the beloved wife of Amenophis.

incitements to monotheism even made their way in from Syria.

Amenophis never denied his adherence to the sun cult of On. In the two Hymns to the Aten which have survived in the rock tombs and which were probably composed by him himself, he praises the sun as the creator and preserver of all living things both inside and outside Egypt with an ardour which is not repeated till many centuries later in the Psalms in honour of the Jewish god Yahweh. He was not content, however, with this astonishing anticipation of the scientific discovery of the effect of solar radiation. There is no doubt that he went a step further: that he did not worship the sun as a material object but as the symbol of a divine being whose energy was manifested in its rays.[1]

We should not, however, be doing justice to the king if we regarded him merely as an adherent or promoter of an Aten religion already in existence before his time. His activity was a far more energetic intervention. He introduced something new, which for the first time converted the doctrine of a universal god into monotheism—the factor of exclusiveness. In one of his hymns he declares expressly: 'O thou sole God, beside whom there is no other!' [2] And we must not forget that in assessing the new doctrine a knowledge of its *positive* contents is not enough: its *negative* side is almost equally important—a knowledge of what it rejects. It would be a mistake, too, to suppose that the new religion was completed at a single blow and sprang to life fully armed, like Athene out of the head of Zeus. Everything suggests, rather, that in the course of the reign of Amenophis it increased little by little to ever greater clarity, consistency, harshness and intolerance. It is likely that this development came about under the influence of the violent opposition to the

[1] 'But, however evident the Heliopolitan origin of the new state religion might be, it was not merely sun-worship; the word Aton was employed in the place of the old word for "god" (*nuter*), and the god is clearly distinguished from the material sun.' Breasted, 1906, 360.—'It is evident that what the king was deifying was the force by which the Sun made himself felt on earth.' Breasted, 1934, 279.—Erman (1905 [66]) makes a similar judgement on a formula in honour of the god: 'These are . . . words which are meant to express as abstractly as possible that it is not the heavenly body itself that is worshipped but the being which reveals itself in it.'

[2] Breasted, 1906, 374 *n*.

king's reform which arose among the priests of Amun. In the sixth year of the reign of Amenophis this antagonism had reached such a pitch that the king changed his name, of which the proscribed name of the god Amun formed a part. Instead of 'Amenophis' he now called himself 'Akhenaten'.[1] But it was not only from his own name that he expunged that of the detested god: he erased it too from every inscription—even where it occurred in the name of his father, Amenophis III. Soon after changing his name Akhenaten abandoned the Amun-dominated city of Thebes and built himself a new royal capital lower down the river, which he named Akhetaten (the horizon of the Aten). Its ruined site is now known as Tell el-'Amarna.[2]

The persecution by the king fell most harshly upon Amun, but not on him alone. Throughout the kingdom temples were closed, divine service forbidden, temple property confiscated. Indeed, the king's zeal went so far that he had the ancient monuments examined in order to have the word 'god' obliterated in them where it occurred in the plural.[3] It is not to be wondered at that these measures taken by Akhenaten provoked a mood of fanatical vindictiveness among the suppressed priesthood and unsatisfied common people, and this was able to find free expression after the king's death. The Aten religion had not become popular; it had probably remained restricted to a narrow circle surrounding the king's person. Akhenaten's end remains veiled in obscurity. We hear of a few short-lived, shadowy successors from his own family. His son-law, Tut'ankhaten, was already compelled to return to Thebes and to replace the name of the god Aten in his name by that of Amun. There followed a period of anarchy till in 1350 B.C.

[1] [In the German editions the name is spelt 'Ikhnaton'.] I adopt here the English spelling of the name (alternatively 'Akhenaton'). The king's new name has approximately the same meaning as his earlier one: 'The god is satisfied.' Cf. the German 'Gotthold' ['God is gracious'] and 'Gottfried' ['God is satisfied'].—[This footnote is translated literally from the German editions. In fact, 'Ikhnaton' was Breasted's (American) version. For all this see the 'Note on the Transcription of Proper Names', p. 6 above.]

[2] It was there that in 1887 the discovery—of such great historical importance—was made of the Egyptian kings' correspondence with their friends and vassals in Asia.

[3] Breasted, 1906, 363.

a general, Haremhab, succeeded in restoring order. The glorious Eighteenth Dynasty was at an end and simultaneously its conquests in Nubia and Asia were lost. During this gloomy interregnum the ancient religions of Egypt were re-established. The Aten religion was abolished, Akhenaten's royal city was destroyed and plundered and his memory proscribed as that of a criminal.

It is with a particular purpose that we shall now emphasize a few points among the negative characteristics of the Aten religion. In the first place, everything to do with myths, magic and sorcery is excluded from it.[1] In the next place, the manner in which the sun-god was represented was no longer, as in the past, by a small pyramid and a falcon,[2] but—and this seems almost prosaic—by a round disk with rays proceeding from it, which end in human hands. In spite of all the exuberant art of the Amarna period, no other representation of the sun-god—no personal image of the Aten—has been found, and it may confidently be said that none will be found.[3] Lastly, there was complete silence about the god of the dead, Osiris, and the kingdom of the dead. Neither the hymns nor the tomb inscriptions have any knowledge of what perhaps lay closest to the hearts of the Egyptians. The contrast to the popular religion cannot be more clearly demonstrated.[4]

(3)

I should now like to venture on this conclusion: if Moses was an Egyptian and if he communicated his own religion to the Jews, it must have been Akhenaten's, the Aten religion.

[1] Weigall (1922, 120–1) says that Akhenaten would hear nothing of a Hell against whose terrors people might protect themselves with innumerable magical formulae: 'Akhnaton flung all these formulae into the fire. Djins, bogies, spirits, monsters, demigods, demons, and Osiris himself with all his court, were swept into the blaze and reduced to ashes.'

[2] [This should perhaps read 'a pyramid or a falcon'. Cf. Breasted, 1934, 278.]

[3] 'Akhnaton did not permit any graven image to be made of the Aton. The True God, said the king, had no form; and he held to this opinion throughout his life.' (Weigall, 1922, 103.)

[4] 'Nothing was to be heard any more of Osiris and his kingdom.' (Erman, 1905, 70.)—'Osiris is completely ignored. He is never mentioned in any record of Ikhnaton or in any of the tombs at Amarna.' (Breasted, 1934, 291.)

I have already compared the Jewish religion with the popular religion of Egypt and shown the opposition between them. I must now make a comparison between the Jewish and the Aten religions in the expectation of proving their original identity. This, I am aware, will present no easy task. Thanks to the vindictiveness of the priests of Amun we may perhaps know too little of the Aten religion. We only know the Mosaic religion in its final shape, as it was fixed by the Jewish priesthood some eight hundred years later in post-exilic times. If, in spite of this unfavourable state of the material, we find a few indications which favour our hypothesis, we shall be able to set a high value on them.

There would be a short path to proving our thesis that the Mosaic religion was none other than that of the Aten—namely, if we had a confession of faith, a declaration. But I fear we shall be told that this path is closed to us. The Jewish confession of faith, as is well known, runs: 'Schema Jisroel Adonai Elohenu Adonai Echod.' [1] If it is not merely by chance that the name of the Egyptian Aten (or Atum) sounds like the Hebrew word *Adonai* [lord] and the name of the Syrian deity Adonis, but if it is due to a primaeval kinship of speech and meaning, then the Jewish formula might be translated thus: 'Hear, o Israel: our god Aten (Adonai) is a sole god.' Unfortunately I am totally incompetent to answer this question, and I have been able to find but little about it in the literature of the subject.[2] But in all probability this is making things too easy for us. In any case we shall have to come back once more to the problems concerning the name of the god.

The similarities as well as the differences between the two religions are easily discernible without giving us much light. Both of them were forms of a strict monotheism, and we shall be inclined *a priori* to trace back what they had in common to this fundamental characteristic. Jewish monotheism behaved in some respects even more harshly than the Egyptian: for instance

[1] ['Hear, o Israel: the Lord our God is one Lord' (*Deuteronomy*, vi, 4).]

[2] Only a few passages in Weigall (1922, 12 and 19), to the effect that 'the god Atum, the aspect of Ra as the setting sun, was probably of common origin with Aton who was largely worshipped in North Syria', and that a 'foreign queen with her retinue may have therefore felt more sympathy with Heliopolis than with Thebes.' [The connection between Aten and Atum, suggested by Weigall, is not generally accepted by Egyptologists.]

in forbidding pictorial representations of any kind. The most essential difference is to be seen (apart from their gods' names) in the fact that the Jewish religion was entirely without sun-worship, in which the Egyptian one still found support. When we were making the comparison with the popular religion of Egypt, we had an impression that, apart from the fundamental contrast, a factor of *intentional* contradiction played a part in the difference between the two religions. This impression seems to be justified if now, in making the comparison, we replace the Jewish religion by the Aten religion which, as we know, was developed by Akhenaten in deliberate hostility to the popular one. We were rightly surprised to find that the Jewish religion would have nothing to do with the next world or a life after death, though a doctrine of that kind would have been compatible with the strictest monotheism. But this surprise vanishes if we turn back from the Jewish to the Aten religion and suppose that this refusal was taken over from it, since for Akhenaten it was a necessity in his fight against the popular religion, in which Osiris, the god of the dead, played a greater part, perhaps, than any god in the upper world. The agreement between the Jewish and the Aten religions on this important point is the first strong argument in favour of our thesis. We shall learn that it is not the only one.

Moses did not only give the Jews a new religion; it can be stated with equal certainty that he introduced the custom of circumcision to them. This fact is of decisive importance for our problem and has scarcely ever been considered. It is true that the Biblical account contradicts this more than once. On the one hand it traces circumcision back to the patriarchal age as a mark of a covenant between God and Abraham; on the other hand it describes in a quite particularly obscure passage how God was angry with Moses for having neglected a custom which had become holy,[1] and sought to kill him; but that his wife, a Midianite, saved her husband from God's wrath by quickly performing the operation.[2] These, however, are distortions, which should not lead us astray; later on we shall discover the reason for them. The fact remains that there is only one answer to the question of where the Jews derived the custom of cir-

[1] ['*Heilig.*' Cf. p. 120.]

[2] [*Genesis*, xvii, 9 ff. and *Exodus*, iv, 24 ff. Cf. the explanation of the episode on p. 44 below.]

cumcision from—namely, from Egypt. Herodotus, the 'father of history', tells us that the custom of circumcision had long been indigenous in Egypt,[1] and his statements are confirmed by the findings in mummies and indeed by pictures on the walls of tombs. No other people of the Eastern Mediterranean, so far as we know, practised this custom; it may safely be presumed that the Semites, Babylonians and Sumerians were uncircumcised. The Bible story itself says this is so of the inhabitants of Canaan; it is a necessary premiss to the adventure of Jacob's daughter and the prince of Shechem.[2] The possibility that the Jews acquired the custom of circumcision during their sojourn in Egypt in some way other than in connection with the religious teaching of Moses may be rejected as completely without foundation. Now, taking it as certain that circumcision was a universal popular custom in Egypt, let us for a moment adopt the ordinary hypothesis that Moses was a Jew, who sought to free his compatriots from bondage in Egypt and lead them to develop an independent and self-conscious national existence in another country—which was what in fact happened. What sense could it have, in that case, that he should at the same time impose on them a troublesome custom which even, to some extent, made them into Egyptians and which must keep permanently alive their memory of Egypt—whereas his efforts could only be aimed in the opposite direction, towards alienating his people from the land of their bondage and overcoming their longing for the 'flesh-pots of Egypt'? No, the fact from which we started and the hypothesis which we added to it are so incompatible with each other that we may be bold enough to reach this conclusion: if Moses gave the Jews not only a new religion but also the commandment for circumcision, he

[1] [Herodotus, *History*, Book II, Chapter 104.]

[2] [*Genesis*, xxxiv.] I am very well aware that in dealing so autocratically and arbitrarily with Biblical tradition—bringing it up to confirm my views when it suits me and unhesitatingly rejecting it when it contradicts me—I am exposing myself to serious methodological criticism and weakening the convincing force of my arguments. But this is the only way in which one can treat material of which one knows definitely that its trustworthiness has been severely impaired by the distorting influence of tendentious purposes. It is to be hoped that I shall find some degree of justification later on, when I come upon the track of these secret motives. Certainty is in any case unattainable and moreover it may be said that every other writer on the subject has adopted the same procedure.

was not a Jew but an Egyptian, and in that case the Mosaic religion was probably an Egyptian one and, in view of its contrast to the popular religion, the religion of the Aten, with which the later Jewish religion agrees in some remarkable respects.

I have pointed out that my hypothesis that Moses was not a Jew but an Egyptian created a fresh riddle. His course of conduct, which seemed easily intelligible in a Jew, was un-understandable in an Egyptian. If, however, we place Moses in the time of Akhenaten and suppose him in contact with that Pharaoh, the riddle vanishes and the possibility is revealed of motives which will answer all our questions. Let us start from the assumption that Moses was an aristocratic and prominent man, perhaps in fact a member of the royal house, as the legend says of him. He was undoubtedly aware of his great capacities, ambitious and energetic; he may even have played with the notion of one day being the leader of his people, of becoming the kingdom's ruler. Being close to the Pharaoh, he was a convinced adherent of the new religion, whose basic thoughts he had made his own. When the king died and the reaction set in, he saw all his hopes and prospects destroyed; if he was not prepared to abjure all the convictions that were so dear to him, Egypt had nothing more to offer him—he had lost his country. In this predicament he found an unusual solution. Akhenaten the dreamer had alienated his people and let his empire fall to pieces. The more energetic nature of Moses was more at home with the plan of founding a new kingdom, of finding a new people to whom he would present for their worship the religion which Egypt had disdained. It was, we can see, a heroic attempt to combat destiny, to compensate in two directions for the losses in which Akhenaten's catastrophe had involved him. Perhaps he was at that time Governor of the frontier province (Goshen) in which certain Semitic tribes had settled (perhaps as early as in the Hyksos period[1]). These he chose to be his new people—a historic decision.[2] He came to an agreement with them, put

[1] [A disordered period some 200 years before the time of Akhenaten, when a Semitic people (the so-called 'Shepherd Kings') ruled Northern Egypt.]

[2] If Moses was a high official, this makes it easier to understand the role of leader which he assumed with the Jews; if he was a priest, then it was natural for him to emerge as the founder of a religion. In both these cases he would have been continuing his former profession. A

himself at their head and carried the Exodus through 'by strength of hand'.[1] In complete contrast to the Biblical tradition, we may presume that this Exodus took place peacefully and unpursued. The authority of Moses made this possible and at that time there was no central administration which might have interfered with it.

According to this construction of ours, the Exodus from Egypt would have occurred during the period between 1358 and 1350 B.C.—that is, after Akhenaten's death and before Haremhab's re-establishment of state authority.[2] The goal of the migration could only have been the land of Canaan. After the collapse of the Egyptian domination, hordes of warlike Aramaeans had irrupted into that region, conquering and plundering, and had shown in that way where a capable people might win fresh land for themselves. We learn of these warriors from the letters found in 1887 in the ruined city of Amarna. There they are called 'Habiru', and the name was transferred (we do not know how) to the later Jewish invaders —'Hebrews'—who cannot be intended in the Amarna letters. South of Palestine, too, in Canaan, there lived the tribes which were the nearest relatives of the Jews who were now making their way out of Egypt.

The motives which we have discovered for the Exodus as a whole apply also to the introduction of circumcision. We are familiar with the attitude adopted by people (both nations and individuals) to this primaeval usage, which is scarcely understood any longer. Those who do not practise it look on it as very strange and are a little horrified by it, but those who have adopted circumcision are proud of it. They feel exalted by it,

prince of the royal house might easily have been both—a provincial governor and a priest. In the account given by Flavius Josephus (in his *Jewish Antiquities*), who accepts the exposure legend but seems to be in touch with traditions other than the Biblical one, Moses, as an Egyptian general, fought a victorious campaign in Ethiopia. [English translation, 1930, 269 ff.]

[1] [*Exodus*, xiii, 3, 14 and 16.]

[2] This would make the Exodus about a century earlier than is supposed by most historians, who put it in the Nineteenth Dynasty under Merenptah [sometimes transliterated 'Meneptah']. Or it may have happened a little later [than is suggested in the text above], for the official [Egyptian] histories seem to have included the interregnum in the reign of Haremhab. [See below, p. 48.]

ennobled, as it were, and look down with contempt on the others, whom they regard as unclean. Even to this day a Turk will abuse a Christian as an 'uncircumcised dog'. It may be supposed that Moses, who, being an Egyptian, was himself circumcised, shared this attitude. The Jews with whom he departed from his country were to serve him as a superior substitute for the Egyptians he had left behind. On no account must the Jews be inferior to them. He wished to make them into a 'holy nation', as is expressly stated in the Biblical text,[1] and as a mark of this consecration he introduced among them too the custom which made them at least the equals of the Egyptians. And he could only welcome it if they were to be isolated by such a sign and kept apart from the foreign peoples among whom their wanderings would lead them, just as the Egyptians themselves had kept apart from all foreigners.[2]

Later on, however, Jewish tradition behaved as though it were put at a disadvantage by the inference we have been drawing. If it were to be admitted that circumcision was an Egyptian custom introduced by Moses, that would be almost as much as to recognize that the religion delivered to them by Moses was an Egyptian one too. There were good reasons for denying that fact, so the truth about circumcision must also be contradicted.

[1] [*Exodus*, xix, 6. The same word is used in this connection elsewhere in the Authorized Version, e.g. *Deuteronomy*, vii, 6. Cf. p. 120.]

[2] Herodotus, who visited Egypt about 450 B.C., enumerates in his account of his journey characteristics of the Egyptian people which exhibit an astonishing similarity to traits familiar to us in later Jewry: 'They are altogether more religious in every respect than any other people, and differ from them too in a number of their customs. Thus they practise circumcision, which they were the first to introduce, and on grounds of cleanliness. Further they have a horror of pigs, which is no doubt related to the fact that Seth in the form of a black pig wounded Horus. And lastly and most markedly, they hold cows in the greatest honour, and would never eat or sacrifice them, because this would offend Isis with her cow's horns. For that reason no Egyptian man or woman would ever kiss a Greek or use his knife or his spit or his cauldron or eat the flesh of an otherwise clean ox if it had been cut with a Greek knife . . . They look down in narrow-minded pride on other people, who are unclean and are not so close to the gods as they are.' (Erman, 1905, 181.) [This is a summary by Erman of Chapters 36 to 47 of Book II of Herodotus.]—We must not, of course, overlook parallels to this in the life of the Indian people.—And, incidentally, who suggested to the Jewish poet Heine in the nineteenth century A.D. that he should complain

(4)

At this point I expect to be met by an objection to my hypothesis. This placed Moses, an Egyptian, in the Akhenaten period. It derived his decision to take over the Jewish people from the political circumstances in the country at that time, and it recognized the religion that he presented to or imposed on his *protégés* as the Aten religion, which had actually collapsed in Egypt itself. I expect to be told that I have brought forward this structure of conjectures with too much positiveness, for which there is no basis in the material. This objection is, I think, unjustified. I have already laid stress on the factor of doubt in my introductory remarks; I have, as it were, placed that factor outside the brackets and I may be allowed to save myself the trouble of repeating it in connection with each item *inside* them.[1]

I may continue the discussion with a few critical remarks of my own. The kernel of my hypothesis—the dependence of Jewish monotheism on the monotheist episode in Egyptian history—has been suspected and mentioned by various writers. I spare myself the trouble of quoting these opinions here, since none of them is able to indicate how this influence can have come into operation. Even though in our view that influence remains linked to the figure of Moses, we ought also to mention some other possibilities in addition to the one we prefer. It must not be supposed that the fall of the official Aten religion brought the monotheist current in Egypt to a complete stop. The priesthood at On, from which it started, survived the catastrophe and may have continued to bring under the sway of its trend of ideas generations after Akhenaten's. Thus the action taken by Moses is still conceivable even if he did not live at the time of Akhenaten and did not fall under his personal influence, if he was only an adherent or perhaps a member of the priesthood of On. This possibility would postpone the date of the Exodus and bring it closer to the date which is usually adopted (in the thirteenth century); but it has nothing else to recommend it. Our insight into the motives of Moses would be lost and the facilitation of the Exodus by the prevailing anarchy in the

of his religion as 'the plague dragged along from the Nile valley, the unhealthy beliefs of Ancient Egypt'? [From a poem on 'The New Jewish Hospital in Hamburg', *Zeitgedichte*, XI.]

[1] [This, of course, is a simile from algebra.]

country would no longer apply. The succeeding kings of the Nineteenth Dynasty established a strong *régime*. It was only during the period immediately after the heretic king's death that there was a convergence of all the conditions, external and internal alike, that were favourable to the Exodus.

The Jews possess a copious literature apart from the Bible, in which the legends and myths are to be found which grew up in the course of centuries round the imposing figure of their first leader and the founder of their religion, and which have both illuminated and obscured it. Scattered in this material there may be fragments of trustworthy tradition for which no room was found in the Pentateuch. A legend of this sort gives an engaging account of how the ambition of the man Moses found expression even in his childhood. Once when Pharaoh had taken him in his arms and playfully lifted him high in the air, the little three-year-old boy snatched the crown from the king's head and put it on his own. This portent alarmed the king, who did not fail to consult his wise men about it.[1] There are stories elsewhere of his victorious military actions as an Egyptian general in Ethiopia, and, in this connection, how he fled from Egypt because he had reason to be afraid of the envy of a party at Court or of Pharaoh himself. The Biblical account itself attributes some features to Moses to which credence may well be given. It describes him as being of an irascible nature, flaring up easily, as when, in indignation, he slew the brutal overseer who was ill-treating a Jewish workman, or when in his anger at the people's apostasy he broke the Tables of the Law which he had brought down from the Mount of God [Sinai];[2] indeed God himself punished him in the end for an impatient deed, but we are not told what it was.[3] Since a trait of this kind is not one that would serve for his glorification, it may perhaps correspond to a historical truth. Nor can the possibility be excluded that some of the character traits which the Jews included in their early picture of their God—describing

[1] This anecdote, in a slightly different form, also appears in Josephus. [*Jewish Antiquities*. English translation, 1930, 265 f.]

[2] [*Exodus*, ii, 11–12; xxxii, 19.]

[3] [If this is a reference to Moses, at the end of his life, not being allowed to enter the Promised Land (*Deuteronomy*, xxxiv, 4), the explanation was in fact that he had shown impatience by striking the rock with his rod to draw water instead of merely speaking to it (*Numbers*, xx, 11–12).]

him as jealous, severe and ruthless—may have been at bottom derived from a recollection of Moses; for in fact it was not an invisible God but the man Moses who brought them out of Egypt.

Another trait attributed to Moses has a special claim to our interest. Moses is said to have been 'slow of speech': he must have suffered from an inhibition or disorder of speech. Consequently, in his supposed dealings with Pharaoh, he needed the support of Aaron, who is called his brother.[1] This again may be a historical truth and would make a welcome contribution to presenting a lively picture of the great man. But it may also have another and more important significance. It may recall, slightly distorted, the fact that Moses spoke another language and could not communicate with his Semitic neo-Egyptians without an interpreter, at all events at the beginning of their relations—a fresh confirmation, then, of the thesis that Moses was an Egyptian.

Now, however, or so it seems, our work has reached a provisional end. For the moment we can draw no further conclusions from our hypothesis that Moses was an Egyptian, whether it has been proved or not. No historian can regard the Biblical account of Moses and the Exodus as anything other than a pious piece of imaginative fiction, which has recast a remote tradition for the benefit of its own tendentious purposes. The original form of that tradition is unknown to us; we should be glad to discover what the distorting purposes were, but we are kept in the dark by our ignorance of the historical events. The fact that our reconstruction leaves no room for a number of show-pieces in the Bible story, such as the ten plagues, the passage of the Red Sea and the solemn law-giving on Mount Sinai—this does not disconcert us. But we cannot treat it as a matter of indifference if we find ourselves in contradiction to the findings of the sober historical researches of the present day.

These modern historians, of whom we may take Eduard Meyer (1906) as a representative, agree with the Bible story on one decisive point. They too are of opinion that the Jewish tribes, which later developed into the people of Israel, took on a new religion at a certain point of time. But in their view this did not take place in Egypt or at the foot of a mountain in the

[1] [*Exodus*, iv, 10 and 14.]

Sinai Peninsula, but in a certain locality known as Meribah-Kadesh,[1] an oasis distinguished by its wealth of springs and wells in the stretch of country south of Palestine, between the eastern exit from the Sinai Peninsula and the western border of Arabia.[2] There they took over the worship of a god Yahweh,[3] probably from the neighbouring Arabian tribe of Midianites. It seems likely that other tribes in the vicinity were also followers of this god.

Yahweh was unquestionably a volcano god. Now, as is well known, Egypt is without volcanoes and the mountains of the Sinai Peninsula have never been volcanic; on the other hand, there are volcanoes which may have been active till recent times along the western border of Arabia. So one of these mountains must have been the Sinai-Horeb which was regarded as the home of Yahweh.[4] In spite of all the revisions to which the Biblical story was subjected, the original picture of the god's character can, according to Eduard Meyer, be reconstructed: he was an uncanny, bloodthirsty demon who went about by night and shunned the light of day.[5]

The mediator between God and the people in the founding of this religion was named Moses. He was the son-in-law of the Midianite priest Jethro, and was keeping his flocks when he received the summons from God. He was also visited by Jethro at Kadesh and given some advice by him.[6]

Though Eduard Meyer says, it is true, that he never doubted that there was some historical core in the story of the sojourn in Egypt and the catastrophe to the Egyptians,[7] he evidently does not know how to place and what use to make of this fact

[1] [Throughout this work Freud uses the more technical phonetic spelling of the latter part of this name: Qadeš. We have adopted the ordinary English version.]

[2] [Its precise position seems uncertain, but it was probably in what is now known as the Negev, on about the same latitude as Petra but some fifty miles further to the West. It is not to be confused with the better-known Kadesh in Syria, to the north of Palestine, which was the scene of a much boasted victory by Ramesses II over the Hittites.]

[3] [This is the usual English spelling. Freud uses the corresponding German one: 'Jahve'.]

[4] At a few places in the Biblical text it is still stated that Yahweh came down from Sinai to Meribah-Kadesh. [E.g. *Numbers*, xx, 6–9.—Sinai and Horeb are usually taken as different names of the same mountain.]

[5] Meyer, 1906, 38 and 58.

[6] [*Exodus*, iii, 1 and xviii, 2–27.]

[7] Meyer, 1906, 49.

which he recognizes. The only thing he is prepared to derive from Egypt is the custom of circumcision. He adds two important indications which go to confirm our previous arguments: first, that Joshua ordered the people to be circumcised in order to 'roll away the reproach [i.e. contempt] of Egypt from off you',[1] and secondly a quotation from Herodotus saying that 'the Phoenicians (no doubt the Jews) and the Syrians of Palestine themselves admit that they learnt the custom of the Egyptians'.[2] But he has little to say in favour of an Egyptian Moses: 'The Moses we know is the ancestor of the priests of Kadesh—that is, a figure from a genealogical legend, standing in relation to a cult, and not a historical personality. Thus (apart from those who accept tradition root and branch as historical truth) no one who treats him as a historical figure has been able to give any content to him, to represent him as a concrete individual or to point out what he may have done and what his historical work may have been.' [3]

On the other hand, Meyer is never tired of insisting on the relation of Moses to Kadesh and Midian: 'The figure of Moses, which is intimately bound up with Midian and the cult-centres in the desert. . . .' [4] and: 'This figure of Moses, then, is inseparably linked with Kadesh (Massah and Meribah[5]) and this is supplemented by his being the son-in-law of the Midianite priest. His link with the Exodus, on the contrary, and the whole story of his youth are entirely secondary and simply the consequence of the interpolation of Moses into a connected and continuous legendary story.'[6] Meyer also points out that the themes included in the story of the youth of Moses were one and all dropped later: 'Moses in Midian is no longer an Egyptian and grandson of Pharaoh, but a shepherd to whom Yahweh revealed himself. In telling of the plagues there is no longer any talk of his former connections, though effective use might easily have been made of them, and the command to kill the [new-born] sons of the Israelites[7] is completely forgotten. In the Exodus and the destruction of the Egyptians

[1] [*Joshua*, v, 9.]

[2] Meyer, 1906, 449. [Quoted from Herodotus, *History*, Book II, Chapter 104.]

[3] Meyer, 1906, 451 [footnote].

[4] Meyer, 1906, 49.

[5] [These seem to be the names of springs at Kadesh. Cf. *Exodus*, xvii, 7.]

[6] Meyer, 1906, 72.

[7] [*Exodus*, i, 16 and 22.]

Moses plays no part whatever: he is not even mentioned. The heroic character which the legend of his childhood presupposes is totally absent from the later Moses; he is only the man of God, a miracle-worker equipped by Yahweh with supernatural powers.' [1]

We cannot dispute the impression that this Moses of Kadesh and Midian, to whom tradition could actually attribute the erection of a brazen serpent as a god of healing,[2] is someone quite other than the aristocratic Egyptian inferred by us, who presented the people with a religion in which all magic and spells were proscribed in the strictest terms. Our Egyptian Moses is no less different, perhaps, from the Midianite Moses than is the universal god Aten from the demon Yahweh in his home on the Mount of God. And if we have any faith at all in the pronouncements of the recent historians, we shall have to admit that the thread which we have tried to spin from our hypothesis that Moses was an Egyptian has broken for the second time. And this time, as it seems, with no hope of mending.

(5)

Unexpectedly, here once more a way of escape presents itself. Efforts to see in Moses a figure that goes beyond the priest of Kadesh, and to confirm the grandeur with which tradition glorifies him, have not ceased even since Eduard Meyer. (Cf. Gressmann [1913] and others.) Then, in 1922, Ernst Sellin made a discovery which affected our problem decisively. He found in the Prophet Hosea (in the second half of the eighth century B.C.) unmistakable signs of a tradition to the effect that Moses, the founder of their religion, met with a violent end in a rising of his refractory and stiff-necked people, and that at the same time the religion he had introduced was thrown off. This tradition is not, however, restricted to Hosea; it reappears in most of the later Prophets, and indeed, according to Sellin, became the basis of all the later Messianic expectations. At the end of the Babylonian captivity a hope grew up among the Jewish people that the man who had been so shamefully murdered would return from the dead and would lead his remorseful people, and perhaps not them alone, into the kingdom of lasting bliss. The obvious connection of this with the

[1] Meyer, 1906, 47.

[2] [*Numbers*, xxi, 9.]

destiny of the founder of a later religion does not concern us here.

Once again I am not, of course, in a position to judge whether Sellin has interpreted the passages from the Prophets correctly. But if he is right we may attribute historical credibility to the tradition he has recognized, for such things are not readily invented. There is no tangible motive for doing so; but if they have really happened, it is easy to understand that people will be anxious to forget them. We need not accept all the details of the tradition. In Sellin's opinion Shittim, in the country east of the Jordan, is to be regarded as the scene of the attack on Moses. But we shall soon see that that region is not acceptable for our notions.

We will borrow from Sellin his hypothesis that the Egyptian Moses was murdered by the Jews and the religion he had introduced abandoned. This allows us to spin our threads further without contradicting the authentic findings of historical research. But apart from this we shall venture to maintain independence of the authorities and to 'proceed along our own track'. The Exodus from Egypt remains our starting-point. A considerable number of people must have left the country with Moses; a small collection would not have seemed worth while to this ambitious man with his large aims in view. The immigrants had probably been living in Egypt long enough to have grown into quite a large population. But we shall certainly not be going wrong if we assume, with the majority of the authorities, that only a fraction of what was later to be the Jewish people had experienced the events in Egypt. In other words, the tribe that returned from Egypt joined up later, in the stretch of country between Egypt and Canaan, with other kindred tribes, which had been settled there for a considerable time. This union, from which sprang the people of Israel, found expression in the adoption of a new religion, common to all the tribes, the religion of Yahweh—an event which, according to Eduard Meyer [1906, 60 ff.], took place under Midianite influence at Kadesh. Thereafter, the people felt strong enough to undertake their invasion of the land of Canaan. It would not tally with this course of events to suppose that the catastrophe to Moses and his religion occurred in the country east of the Jordan; it must have happened long before the union of the tribes.

There can be no doubt that very different elements came together in the construction of the Jewish people; but what must have made the greatest difference among these tribes was whether they had experienced or not the sojourn in Egypt and what followed it. Having regard to this point, we may say that the nation arose out of a union of two component parts; and it fits in with this that, after a short period of political unity, it split into two pieces—the kingdom of Israel and the kingdom of Judah. History is fond of reinstatements like this, where a later fusion is undone and an earlier separation re-emerges. The most impressive example of this was afforded, as is well known, by the Reformation, which, after an interval of over a thousand years, brought to light once more the frontier between the Germany which had at one time been Roman and the Germany which had remained independent. In the instance of the Jewish people it is not possible to point to such a faithful reproduction of the old state of things; our knowledge of those times is too uncertain to allow us to assert that the settled tribes were once more to be found together in the Northern Kingdom and those who had returned from Egypt in the Southern Kingdom; but here too the later split cannot have been unrelated to the earlier joining up. The former Egyptians were probably fewer in numbers than the others, but showed themselves culturally the stronger. They exercised a more powerful influence on the further evolution of the people, because they brought along with them a tradition which the others lacked.

Perhaps they brought something else with them more tangible than a tradition. One of the greatest enigmas of Jewish prehistory is that of the origin of the Levites. They are traced back to one of the twelve tribes of Israel—that of Levi—but no tradition has ventured to say where that tribe was originally located or what portion of the conquered land of Canaan was allotted to it. They filled the most important priestly offices, but they were distinct from the priests. A Levite is not necessarily a priest; nor is it the name of a caste. Our hypothesis about the figure of Moses suggests an explanation. It is incredible that a great lord, like Moses the Egyptian, should have joined this alien people unaccompanied. He certainly must have brought a retinue with him—his closest followers, his scribes, his domestic servants. This is who the Levites originally were. The tradition which alleges that Moses was a Levite seems to be a clear distortion of the fact: the Levites were the followers of Moses. This solution is supported by the fact which I have already mentioned in my earlier essay that it is only among the Levites that Egyptian names occur later.[1] It is to be presumed that a fair number of these followers of Moses escaped the catastrophe which descended on him himself and the religion he founded. They multiplied in the course of the next generations, became fused with the people they lived among, but remained loyal to their master, preserved his memory and carried out the tradition of his doctrines. At the time of the union with the disciples of Yahweh they formed an influential minority, culturally superior to the rest.

I put it forward as a provisional hypothesis that between the fall of Moses and the establishment of the new religion at Kadesh two generations, or perhaps even a century, elapsed. I see no means of deciding whether the Neo-Egyptians (as I should like to call them here)—that is, those who returned from Egypt—met their tribal kinsmen after the latter had already adopted the Yahweh religion or earlier. The second possibility might seem the more probable. But there would be no difference in the outcome. What happened at Kadesh was a compromise, in which the share taken by the tribes of Moses is unmistakable.

Here we may once again call on the evidence afforded by circumcision, which has repeatedly been of help to us, like, as it were, a key-fossil. This custom became obligatory in the Yahweh religion as well and, since it was indissolubly linked with Egypt, its adoption can only have been a concession to the followers of Moses, who—or the Levites among them—would not renounce this mark of their holiness. [P. 30.] So much of their old religion they wished to rescue, and in return for it they were prepared to accept the new deity and what the priests of Midian told them about it. They may possibly have gained yet other concessions. We have already mentioned that Jewish ritual prescribed certain restrictions on the use of God's name. Instead of 'Yahweh' the word 'Adonai [Lord]' must be spoken. It is tempting to bring this prescription into our context, but

[1] [This earlier mention is not to be found. It was no doubt dropped in the course of Freud's revisions of the book. See, however, an Editor's addition to a footnote on p. 15.] My hypothesis fits in well with Yahuda's statements on the Egyptian influence on early Jewish literature. See Yahuda, 1929.

that is only a conjecture without any other basis. The prohibition upon a god's name is, as is well known, a taboo of primaeval age. We do not understand why it was revived precisely in the Jewish Law; it is not impossible that this happened under the influence of a fresh motive. There is no need to suppose that the prohibition was carried through consistently; in the construction of theophorous personal names—that is, in compounds—the name of the God Yahweh might be freely used (e.g. Jochanan, Jehu, Joshua). There were, however, special circumstances connected with this name. As we know, critical Biblical research supposes that the Hexateuch has two documentary sources.[1] These are distinguished as J and E, because one of them uses 'Jahve [Yahweh]' as the name of God and the other 'Elohim': 'Elohim', to be sure, not 'Adonai'. But we may bear in mind a remark by one of our authorities: 'The different names are a clear indication of two originally different gods.' [2]

We brought up the retention of circumcision as evidence for the fact that the founding of the religion at Kadesh involved a compromise. We can see its nature from the concordant accounts given by J and E, which thus go back on this point to a common source (a documentary or oral tradition). Its leading purpose was to demonstrate the greatness and power of the new god Yahweh. Since the followers of Moses attached so much value to their experience of the Exodus from Egypt, this act of liberation had to be represented as due to Yahweh, and the event was provided with embellishments which gave proof of the terrifying grandeur of the volcano god—such as the pillar of smoke [cloud] which changed at night into a pillar of fire and the storm which laid bare the bed of the sea for a while, so that the pursuers were drowned by the returning waters.[3] This account brought the Exodus and the founding of the religion close together, and disavowed the long interval between them. So, too, the law-giving was represented as occurring not at Kadesh but at the foot of the Mount of God, marked by a volcanic eruption. This account, however, did grave injustice to the memory of the man Moses; it was he and not the volcano god who had liberated the people from Egypt. So a compensation was owing to him, and it consisted in the man Moses being transferred to Kadesh or to Sinai-Horeb and put in the place of

[1] [This is elaborated on p. 42 below.]

[2] Gressmann, 1913, 54.

[3] [*Exodus*, xiii, 21 and xiv, 21–8.]

the Midianite priests. We shall find later that this solution satisfied another imperatively pressing purpose. In this manner a mutual agreement, as it were, was arrived at: Yahweh, who lived on a mountain in Midian, was allowed to extend over into Egypt, and, in exchange for this, the existence and activity of Moses were extended to Kadesh and as far as the country east of the Jordan. Thus he was fused with the figure of the later religious founder, the son-in-law of the Midianite Jethro [p. 35], and lent him his name of Moses. Of this second Moses, however, we can give no personal account—so completely was he eclipsed by the first, the Egyptian Moses—unless we pick out the contradictions in the Biblical description of the character of Moses. He is often pictured as domineering, hot-tempered and even violent, yet he is also described as the mildest and most patient of men.[1] These last qualities would evidently have fitted in badly with the Egyptian Moses, who had to deal with his people in such great and difficult matters; they may have belonged to the character of the other Moses, the Midianite. We are, I think, justified in separating the two figures and in assuming that the Egyptian Moses was never at Kadesh and had never heard the name of Yahweh, and that the Midianite Moses had never been in Egypt and knew nothing of Aten. In order to solder the two figures together, tradition or legend had the task of bringing the Egyptian Moses to Midian, and we have seen that more than one explanation of this was current.

(6)

Once again I am prepared to find myself blamed for having presented my reconstruction of the early history of the people of Israel with too great and unjustified certainty. I shall not feel very severely hit by this criticism, since it finds an echo in my own judgement. I know myself that my structure has its weak spots, but it has its strong points too. On the whole my predominant impression is that it is worth while to pursue the work in the direction it has taken.

The Bible narrative that we have before us contains precious and, indeed, invaluable historical data, which, however, have been distorted by the influence of powerful tendentious purposes and embellished by the products of poetic invention. In the

[1] [See, for instance, *Exodus*, xxxii, 19 and *Numbers*, xii, 3.]

course of our efforts so far, we have been able to detect one of these distorting purposes [p. 40]. That discovery points our further path. We must uncover other similar tendentious purposes. If we find means of recognizing the distortions produced by those purposes, we shall bring to light fresh fragments of the true state of things lying behind them.

And we will begin by listening to what critical Biblical research is able to tell us about the history of the origin of the Hexateuch, the five books of Moses and the book of Joshua, which alone concern us here.[1] The earliest documentary source is accepted as J (the Yahwistic writer), who in the most recent times has been identified as the priest Ebyatar, a contemporary of King David.[2] Somewhat—it is not known how much—later we come to the so-called Elohistic writer [E], who belonged to the Northern Kingdom.[3] After the collapse of the Northern Kingdom in 722 B.C., a Jewish priest combined portions of J and E and made some additions of his own. His compilation is designated as JE. In the seventh century *Deuteronomy*, the fifth book, was added to this. It is supposed to have been found complete in the Temple. In the period after the destruction of the Temple (586 B.C.), during and after the Exile, the revision known as the 'Priestly Code' was compiled; and in the fifth century the work was given its final revision and since then has not been changed in its essentials.[4]

The history of King David and of his period is most probably the work of a contemporary. It is genuine historical writing,

[1] *Encyclopaedia Britannica*, Eleventh Edition [Vol. III], 1910. Article 'Bible'.

[2] See Auerbach (1932).

[3] The Yahwistic and Elohistic writings were first distinguished by Astruc in 1753. [Jean Astruc (1684–1766) was a French physician attached to the Court of Louis XV.]

[4] It is historically certain that the Jewish type was finally fixed as a result of the reforms of Ezra and Nehemiah in the fifth century before Christ—that is, after the Exile, under the Persian domination which was friendly to the Jews. On our reckoning, some nine hundred years had passed since the emergence of Moses. These reforms took seriously the regulations that aimed at making the entire people holy; their separation from their neighbours was made effective by the prohibition of mixed marriages; the Pentateuch, the true book of the laws, was given its final form and the revision known as the Priestly Code brought to completion. It seems certain, however, that these reforms introduced no fresh tendentious purposes, but took up and strengthened earlier trends.

five hundred years before Herodotus, the 'father of History'. It becomes easier to understand this achievement if, on the lines of our hypothesis, we think of Egyptian influence.[1] A suspicion even arises that the Israelites of that earliest period—that is to say, the scribes of Moses—may have had some share in the invention of the first alphabet.[2] It is, of course, beyond our knowledge to discover how far reports about former times go back to early records or to oral tradition and how long an interval of time there was in individual instances between an event and its recording. The text, however, as we possess it to-day, will tell us enough about its own vicissitudes. Two mutually opposed treatments have left their traces on it. On the one hand it has been subjected to revisions which have falsified it in the sense of their secret aims, have mutilated and amplified it and have even changed it into its reverse; on the other hand a solicitous piety has presided over it and has sought to preserve everything as it was, no matter whether it was consistent or contradicted itself. Thus almost everywhere noticeable gaps, disturbing repetitions and obvious contradictions have come about—indications which reveal things to us which it was not intended to communicate. In its implications the distortion of a text resembles a murder: the difficulty is not in perpetrating the deed, but in getting rid of its traces. We might well lend the word '*Entstellung* [distortion]' the double meaning to which it has a claim but of which to-day it makes no use. It should mean not only 'to change the appearance of something' but also 'to put something in another place, to displace'.[3] Accordingly, in many instances of textual distortion, we may nevertheless count upon finding what has been suppressed and disavowed hidden away somewhere else, though changed and torn from its context. Only it will not always be easy to recognize it.

The distorting purposes which we are anxious to lay hold of must have been at work already on the traditions before any of them were committed to writing. We have already discovered

[1] Cf. Yahuda, 1929.

[2] If they were subject to the prohibition against pictures they would even have had a motive for abandoning the hieroglyphic picture-writing while adapting its written characters to expressing a new language. (Cf. Auerbach, 1932, 142) [Hieroglyphic writing included both signs depicting objects and signs representing sounds.]

[3] ['*Stelle*' means 'a place', and '*ent-*' is a prefix indicating a change of condition.]

one of them, perhaps the most powerful of all. As we have said, with the setting-up of the new god, Yahweh, at Kadesh, it became necessary to do something to glorify him. It would be more correct to say: it became necessary to fit him in, to make room for him, to wipe out the traces of earlier religions. This seems to have been achieved with complete success as regards the religion of the resident tribes: we hear nothing more of it. With those returning from Egypt it was not such an easy matter; they would not let themselves be deprived of the Exodus, the man Moses or circumcision. It is true that they had been in Egypt, but they had left it, and thenceforward every trace of Egyptian influence was to be disavowed. The man Moses was dealt with by shifting him to Midian and Kadesh, and by fusing him with the priest of Yahweh who founded the religion. Circumcision, the most suspicious indication of dependence on Egypt, had to be retained but no attempts were spared to detach the custom from Egypt—all evidence to the contrary. It is only as a deliberate denial of the betraying fact that we can explain the puzzling and incomprehensibly worded passage in *Exodus* [iv, 24–6], according to which on one occasion Yahweh was angry with Moses because he had neglected circumcision, and his Midianite wife saved his life by quickly carrying out the operation.[1] We shall presently come across another invention for making the uncomfortable piece of evidence harmless.

The fact that we find signs of efforts being made to deny explicitly that Yahweh was a new god, alien to the Jews, can scarcely be described as the appearance of a fresh tendentious purpose: it is rather a continuation of the former one. With this end in view the legends of the patriarchs of the people—Abraham, Isaac and Jacob—were introduced. Yahweh asserted that he was already the god of these forefathers; though it is true that he himself had to admit that they had not worshipped him under that name.[2] He does not add, however, what the other name was.

And here was the opportunity for a decisive blow against the Egyptian origin of the custom of circumcision: Yahweh, it was said, had already insisted on it with Abraham and had

[1] [Cf. p. 26.]

[2] [Cf. *Exodus*, vi, 3.] This does not make the restrictions upon the use of this new name more intelligible, though it does make them more suspect.

introduced it as the token of the covenant between him and Abraham.[1] But this was a particularly clumsy invention. As a mark that is to distinguish one person from others and prefer him to them, one would choose something that is not to be found in other people; one would *not* choose something that can be exhibited in the same way by millions of other people. An Israelite who was transplanted to Egypt would have had to acknowledge every Egyptian as a brother in the covenant, a brother in Yahweh. It is impossible that the Israelites who created the text of the Bible can have been ignorant of the fact that circumcision was indigenous in Egypt. The passage in Joshua [v, 9] quoted by Eduard Meyer [see p. 35 above] admits this without question; but for that very reason it had to be disavowed at any price.

We must not expect the mythical structures of religion to pay too much attention to logical coherence. Otherwise popular feeling might have taken justified offence against a deity who made a covenant with their forefathers with mutual obligations and then, for centuries on end, paid no attention to his human partners, till it suddenly occurred to him to manifest himself anew to their descendants. Even more puzzling is the notion of a god's all at once 'choosing' a people, declaring them to be his people and himself to be their god. I believe this is the only instance of its sort in the history of human religions. Ordinarily god and people are indissolubly linked, they are one from the very beginning of things. No doubt we sometimes hear of a people taking on a different god, but never of a god seeking a different people. We may perhaps understand this unique event better if we recall the relations between Moses and the Jewish people. Moses had stooped to the Jews, had made them his people: they were his 'chosen people'.[2]

[1] [*Genesis*, xvii, 9–14.]

[2] Yahweh was undoubtedly a volcano god. There was no occasion for the inhabitants of Egypt to worship him. I am certainly not the first person to be struck by the resemblance of the sound of the name 'Yahweh' to the root of the other divine name 'Jupiter (Jove)'. [The letter 'j' in German is pronounced like the English 'y'.] The name 'Jochanan' is compounded with an abbreviation of the Hebrew Yahweh —in the same kind of way as [the German] 'Gotthold [God is gracious]' and the Carthaginian equivalent 'Hannibal'. This name (Jochanan), in the forms 'Johann', 'John', 'Jean', 'Juan', has become the favourite first name in European Christendom. The Italians, in rendering it

The bringing-in of the patriarchs served yet another purpose. They had lived in Canaan, and their memory was linked with particular localities in that country. It is possible that they were themselves originally Canaanite heroes or local divinities, and were then seized on by the immigrant Israelites for their pre-history. By appealing to the patriarchs they were as it were asserting their indigenous character and defending themselves from the odium attaching to an alien conqueror. It was a clever twist to declare that the god Yahweh was only giving them back what their forefathers had once possessed.

In the later contributions to the text of the Bible the intention was put into effect of avoiding the mention of Kadesh. The place at which the religion was founded was fixed once and for all as the Mount of God, Sinai-Horeb. It is not easy to see the motive for this; perhaps people were unwilling to be reminded of the influence of Midian. But all later distortions, especially of the period of the Priestly Code, had another aim in view. There was no longer any need to alter accounts of events in a desired sense—for this had been done long before. But care was taken to shift back commands and institutions of the present day into early times—to base them, as a rule, on the Mosaic law-giving—so as to derive from this their claim to being holy

'Giovanni' and moreover calling a day of the week 'Giovedi [Thursday]', are bringing to light a resemblance which may possibly mean nothing or possibly a very great deal. At this point, extensive but very uncertain prospects open up before us. It seems that, in those obscure centuries which are scarcely accessible to historical research, the countries round the eastern basin of the Mediterranean were the scene of frequent and violent volcanic eruptions, which must have made the strongest impression on their inhabitants. Evans assumes that the final destruction of the palace of Minos at Knossos too was the consequence of an earthquake. In Crete at that period (as probably in the Aegean world in general) the great mother-goddess was worshipped. The realization that she was not able to protect her house against the assaults of a stronger power may have contributed to her having to give place to a male deity, and, if so, the volcano god had the first claim to take her place. After all, Zeus always remains the 'earth-shaker'. There is little doubt that it was during those obscure ages that the mother-goddesses were replaced by male gods (who may originally perhaps have been sons). The destiny of Pallas Athene, who was no doubt the local form of the mother-goddess, is particularly impressive. She was reduced to being a daughter by the religious revolution, she was robbed of her own mother and, by having virginity imposed on her, was permanently excluded from motherhood. [On the mother-goddesses, see below, pp. 83–4.]

and binding. However much the picture of the past might in this way be falsified, the procedure was not without a certain psychological justification. It reflected the fact that in the course of long ages—between the Exodus from Egypt and the fixing of the text of the Bible under Ezra and Nehemiah some eight hundred years elapsed—the Yahweh religion had had its form changed back into conformity, or even perhaps into identity, with the original religion of Moses.

And this is the essential outcome, the momentous substance, of the history of the Jewish religion.

(7)

Of all the events of early times which later poets, priests and historians undertook to work over, one stood out, the suppression of which was enjoined by the most immediate and best human motives. This was the murder of Moses, the great leader and liberator, which Sellin discovered from hints in the writings of the Prophets. Sellin's hypothesis cannot be called fantastic—it is probable enough. Moses, deriving from the school of Akhenaten, employed no methods other than did the king; he commanded, he forced his faith upon the people.[1] The doctrine of Moses may have been even harsher than that of his master. He had no need to retain the sun-god as a support: the school of On had no significance for his alien people. Moses, like Akhenaten, met with the same fate that awaits all enlightened despots. The Jewish people under Moses were just as little able to tolerate such a highly spiritualized[2] religion and find satisfaction of their needs in what it had to offer as had been the Egyptians of the Eighteenth Dynasty. The same thing happened in both cases: those who had been dominated and kept in want rose and threw off the burden of the religion that had been imposed on them. But while the tame Egyptians waited till fate had removed the sacred figure of their Pharaoh, the savage Semites took fate into their own hands and rid themselves of their tyrant.[3]

[1] At that period any other method of influencing them was scarcely possible.

[2] ['*Vergeistigte.*' See below, Essay III, Part II (C) and p. 86, footnote.]

[3] It is really remarkable how little we hear in the thousands of years of Egyptian history of the violent removal or murder of a Pharaoh. A

Nor can it be maintained that the surviving text of the Bible gives us no warning of such an end to Moses. The account of the 'wandering in the wilderness',[1] which may stand for the period during which Moses ruled, describes a succession of serious revolts against his authority which were also, by Yahweh's command, suppressed with bloody punishment. It is easy to imagine that one such rebellion ended in a way different from what the text suggests. The people's defection from the new religion is also described in the text—only as an episode, it is true: namely in the story of the golden calf. In this, by an ingenious turn, the breaking of the tables of the law (which is to be understood symbolically: 'he has broken the law') is transposed on to Moses himself, and his furious indignation is assigned as its motive.[2]

There came a time when people began to regret the murder of Moses and to seek to forget it. This was certainly so at the time of the union of the two portions of the people at Kadesh. But when the Exodus and the foundation of the religion at the oasis [of Kadesh] were brought closer together [p. 40], and Moses was represented as being concerned in the latter instead of the other man [the Midianite priest], not only were the demands of the followers of Moses satisfied but the distressing fact of his violent end was successfully disavowed. In actual fact it is most unlikely that Moses could have taken part in the proceedings at Kadesh even if his life had not been cut short.

We must now make an attempt at elucidating the chronological relations of these events. We have put the Exodus in the period after the end of the Eighteenth Dynasty (1350 B.C.). It may have occurred then or a little later, since the Egyptian chroniclers have included the succeeding years of anarchy in the reign of Haremhab, which brought them to an end and lasted till 1315 B.C. The next (but also the only) fixed point for the chronology is afforded by the stela of [the Pharaoh] Merenptah (1225–15 B.C.), which boasts of his victory over Isiraal (Israel) and the laying waste of her seed (?). The sense to be attached to this inscription is unfortunately doubtful, it is

comparison with Assyrian history, for instance, must increase our surprise at this. It may, of course, be accounted for by the fact that Egyptian history was entirely written to serve official ends.

[1] [*Numbers*, xiv, 33.] [2] [*Exodus*, xxxii, 19.]

supposed to prove that the Israelite tribes were already at that time settled in Canaan.[1] Eduard Meyer rightly concludes from this stela that Merenptah cannot have been the Pharaoh of the Exodus, as had been lightly assumed previously. The date of the Exodus must have been earlier. The question of who was the Pharaoh of the Exodus seems to me altogether an idle one. There was no Pharaoh of the Exodus, for it occurred during an interregnum. Nor does the discovery of the stela of Merenptah throw any light on the possible date of the union and founding of the religion at Kadesh. All that we can say with certainty is that it was some time between 1350 and 1215 B.C. We suspect that the Exodus comes somewhere very near the beginning of this hundred years and the events at Kadesh not too far away from its end. We should like to claim the greater part of this period for the interval between the two occurrences. For we need a comparatively long time for the passions of the returning tribes to have cooled down after the murder of Moses and for the influence of his followers, the Levites, to have become as great as is implied by the compromise at Kadesh. Two generations, sixty years, might about suffice for this, but it is a tight fit. What is inferred from the stela of Merenptah comes too early for us, and since we recognize that in this hypothesis of ours one supposition is only based on another, we must admit that this discussion reveals a weak side of our construction. It is unlucky that everything relating to the settlement of the Jewish people in Canaan is so obscure and confused. Our only resort, perhaps, is to suppose that the name on the 'Israel' stela does not relate to the tribes whose fortunes we are trying to follow and which combined to form the later people of Israel. After all, the name of 'Habiru' (Hebrews) was transferred to these same people in the Amarna period [p. 29].

The union of the tribes into a nation through the adoption of a common religion, whenever it may have taken place, might easily have turned out quite an unimportant happening in world history. The new religion would have been carried away by the current of events, Yahweh would have had to take his place in the procession of departed gods in Flaubert's vision,[2] and all twelve of his tribes would have been 'lost' and not only the ten of them which the Anglo-Saxons have been in search of

[1] Eduard Meyer, 1906, 222 ff.

[2] [In *La tentation de Saint Antoine*, Part V of the final version (1874).]

for so long. The god Yahweh, to whom the Midianite Moses then presented a new people, was probably in no respect a prominent being. A coarse, narrow-minded, local god, violent and bloodthirsty, he had promised his followers to give them 'a land flowing with milk and honey' [1] and urged them to exterminate its present inhabitants 'with the edge of the sword'.[2] It is astonishing how much remains, in spite of all the revisions of the Biblical narratives, that allows us to recognize his original nature. It is not even certain that his religion was a genuine monotheism, that it denied the divinity of the deities of other peoples. It was enough probably that his people regarded their own god as more powerful than any foreign god. If, nevertheless, in the sequel everything took a different course from what such beginnings would have led one to expect, the cause can be found in only one fact. The Egyptian Moses had given to one portion of the people a more highly spiritualized notion of god, the idea of a single deity embracing the whole world, who was not less all-loving than all-powerful, who was averse to all ceremonial and magic and set before men as their highest aim a life in truth and justice. For, however incomplete may be the accounts we have of the ethical side of the Aten religion, it can be no unimportant fact that Akhenaten regularly referred to himself in his inscriptions as 'living in Ma'at' (truth, justice).[3] In the long run it made no difference that the people rejected the teaching of Moses (probably after a short time) and killed him himself. The *tradition* of it remained and its influence achieved (only gradually, it is true, in the course of centuries) what was denied to Moses himself. The god Yahweh had arrived at undeserved honour when, from the time of Kadesh onwards, he was credited with the deed of liberation which had been performed by Moses; but he had to pay heavily for this usurpation. The shadow of the god whose place he had taken became stronger than himself; by the end of the process of evolution, the nature of the forgotten god of Moses had come to light behind his own. No one can doubt that it was only the idea of this other god that enabled the people of Israel to

[1] [*Exodus*, iii, 8.]

[2] [*Deuteronomy*, xiii, 15.]

[3] His hymns lay stress not only on the god's universality and oneness, but also on his loving care for all creatures; and they encourage joy in nature and enjoyment of its beauty. (Breasted, 1934, [281–302].)

survive all the blows of fate and that kept them alive to our own days.

It is no longer possible to estimate the share taken by the Levites in the final victory of the Mosaic god over Yahweh. They had taken the side of Moses in the past, when the compromise was reached at Kadesh, in a still live memory of the master whose retinue and compatriots they had been. During the centuries since then they had become merged with the people or with the priesthood, and it had become the main function of the priests to develop and supervise the ritual, and besides this to preserve the holy writ and revise it in accordance with their aims. But was not all sacrifice and all ceremonial at bottom only magic and sorcery, such as had been unconditionally rejected by the old Mosaic teaching? Thereupon there arose from among the midst of the people an unending succession of men who were not linked to Moses in their origin but were enthralled by the great and mighty tradition which had grown up little by little in obscurity: and it was these men, the Prophets, who tirelessly preached the old Mosaic doctrine—that the deity disdained sacrifice and ceremonial and asked only for faith and a life in truth and justice (Ma'at). The efforts of the Prophets had a lasting success; the doctrines with which they re-established the old faith became the permanent content of the Jewish religion. It is honour enough to the Jewish people that they could preserve such a tradition and produce men who gave it a voice—even though the intiative to it came from outside, from a great foreigner.

I should not feel secure in giving this account, if I could not appeal to the judgement of other enquirers with a specialist knowledge who see the significance of Moses for the Jewish religion in the same light as I do, even though they do not recognize his Egyptian origin. Thus, for instance, Sellin (1922, 52) writes: 'Consequently we must picture the true religion of Moses—his belief in the one moral God whom he preaches—as thenceforward necessarily the property of a small circle of the people. We must necessarily not expect to meet with it in the official cult, in the religion of the priests or in the beliefs of the people. We can necessarily only reckon to find an occasional spark emerging, now here and now there, from the spiritual torch which he once kindled, to find that his ideas have not entirely perished but have been silently at work here and there upon beliefs and customs, till sooner or later, through the effect of special experiences or of persons specially moved by his spirit, it has broken out more strongly once more and gained influence on wider masses of the population. It is from this point of view that the history of the ancient religion of Israel is necessarily to be regarded. Anyone who sought to construct the Mosaic religion on the lines of the religion we meet with, according to the chronicles, in the life of the people during their first five hundred years in Canaan, would be committing the gravest methodological error.' Volz (1907, 64) speaks even more clearly: it is his belief that 'the exalted work of Moses was understood and carried through to begin with only feebly and scantily, till, in the course of centuries, it penetrated more and more, and at length in the great Prophets it met with like spirits who continued the lonely man's work.'

And here, it seems, I have reached the conclusion of my study, which was directed to the single aim of introducing the figure of an Egyptian Moses into the nexus of Jewish history. Our findings may be thus expressed in the most concise formula. Jewish history is familiar to us for its dualities: *two* groups of people who came together to form the nation, *two* kingdoms into which this nation fell apart, *two* gods' names in the documentary sources of the Bible. To these we add two fresh ones: the foundation of *two* religions—the first repressed by the second but nevertheless later emerging victoriously behind it, and *two* religious founders, who are both called by the same name of Moses and whose personalities we have to distinguish from each other. All of these dualities are the necessary consequences of the first one: the fact that one portion of the people had an experience which must be regarded as traumatic and which the other portion escaped. Beyond this there would be a very great deal to discuss, to explain and to assert. Only thus would an interest in our purely historical study find its true justification. What the real nature of a tradition resides in, and what its special power rests on, how impossible it is to dispute the personal influence upon world-history of individual great men, what sacrilege one commits against the splendid diversity of human life if one recognizes only those motives which arise from material needs, from what sources some ideas (and particularly religious ones) derive their power to subject both men and peoples to their yoke—to study all this in the special case of Jewish history would be an alluring task. To continue my work on such lines as these would be to find a link with the statements I put forward twenty-five years ago in *Totem and Taboo* [1912–1913]. But I no longer feel that I have the strength to do so.

III

MOSES, HIS PEOPLE AND MONOTHEIST RELIGION

PART I

Prefatory Note I

([Vienna], before March, 1938)

With the audacity of one who has little or nothing to lose, I propose for a second time to break a well-grounded intention and to add to my two essays on Moses in *Imago*[1] the final portion which I have held back. I ended the last essay with an assertion that I knew my strength would not be enough for this. By that I meant, of course, the weakening of creative powers which goes along with old age;[2] but I was thinking of another obstacle as well.

We are living in a specially remarkable period. We find to our astonishment that progress has allied itself with barbarism. In Soviet Russia they have set about improving the living conditions of some hundred millions of people who were held firmly in subjection. They have been rash enough to withdraw the 'opium' of religion from them and have been wise enough to give them a reasonable amount of sexual liberty; but at the same time they have submitted them to the most cruel coercion and robbed them of any possibility of freedom of thought. With similar violence, the Italian people are being trained up to orderliness and a sense of duty. We feel it as a relief from an oppressive apprehension when we see in the case of the German people that a relapse into almost prehistoric barbarism can occur as well without being attached to any progressive ideas.

[1] [Essays I and II above.]

[2] I do not share the opinion of my contemporary Bernard Shaw, that human beings would only achieve anything good if they could live to be three hundred years old. A prolongation of life would achieve nothing unless many other fundamental changes were to be made in the conditions of life. [Cf. Shaw's *Back to Methuselah*.]

In any case, things have so turned out that to-day the conservative democracies have become the guardians of cultural advance and that, strange to say, it is precisely the institution of the Catholic Church which puts up a powerful defence against the spread of this danger to civilization—the Church which has hitherto been the relentless foe to freedom of thought and to advances towards the discovery of the truth!

We are living here in a Catholic country under the protection of that Church, uncertain how long that protection will hold out. But so long as it lasts, we naturally hesitate to do anything that would be bound to arouse the Church's hostility. This is not cowardice, but prudence. The new enemy, to whom we want to avoid being of service, is more dangerous than the old one with whom we have already learnt to come to terms. The psycho-analytic researches which we carry on are in any case viewed with suspicious attention by Catholicism. I will not maintain that this is unjustly so. If our work leads us to a conclusion which reduces religion to a neurosis of humanity and explains its enormous power in the same way as a neurotic compulsion in our individual patients, we may be sure of drawing the resentment of our ruling powers down upon us. Not that I should have anything to say that would be new or that I did not say clearly a quarter of a century ago:[1] but it has been forgotten in the meantime and it could not be without effect if I repeated it to-day and illustrated it from an example which offers a standard for all religious foundations. It would probably lead to our being prohibited from practising psycho-analysis. Such violent methods of suppression are, indeed, by no means alien to the Church; the fact is rather that it feels it as an invasion of its privileges if someone else makes use of those methods. But psycho-analysis, which in the course of my long life has gone everywhere, still possesses no home that could be more valuable for it than the city in which it was born and grew up.

I do not only think but I *know* that I shall let myself be deterred by this second obstacle, by the external danger, from publishing the last portion of my study on Moses. I have made yet another attempt to get the difficulty out of the way, by telling myself that my fears are based on an over-estimation of

[1] [In *Totem and Taboo* (1912–13).]

my own personal importance: that it will probably be a matter of complete indifference to the authorities what I choose to write about Moses and the origin of monotheist religions. But I feel uncertain in my judgement of this. It seems to me much more possible that malice and sensationalism will counterbalance any lack of recognition of me in the contemporary world's judgement. So I shall not give this work to the public. But that need not prevent my writing it. Especially as I have written it down already once, two years ago,[1] so that I have only to revise it and attach it to the two essays that have preceded it. It may then be preserved in concealment till some day the time arrives when it may venture without danger into the light, or till someone who has reached the same conclusions and opinions can be told: 'there was someone in darker times who thought the same as you!'

[1] [Freud seems in fact to have written it originally *four* years previously, in 1934, and perhaps to have given it a first major revision in 1936. See above, pp. 3–4.]

Prefatory Note II

([London], June, 1938)

The quite special difficulties which have weighed on me during my composition of this study relating to the figure of Moses—internal doubts as well as external obstacles—have resulted in this third and concluding essay being introduced by two different prefaces, which contradict each other and indeed cancel each other out. For in the short space of time between the two there has been a fundamental change in the author's circumstances. At the earlier date I was living under the protection of the Catholic Church, and was afraid that the publication of my work would result in the loss of that protection and would conjure up a prohibition upon the work of the adherents and students of psycho-analysis in Austria. Then, suddenly, came the German invasion and Catholicism proved, to use the words of the Bible, 'a broken reed'. In the certainty that I should now be persecuted not only for my line of thought but also for my 'race'—accompanied by many of my friends, I left the city which, from my early childhood, had been my home for seventy-eight years.

I met with the friendliest reception in lovely, free, magnanimous England. Here I now live, a welcome guest; I can breathe a sigh of relief now that the weight has been taken off me and that I am once more able to speak and write—I had almost said 'and think'—as I wish or as I must. I venture to bring the last portion of my work before the public.

There are no external obstacles remaining, or at least none to be frightened of. In the few weeks of my stay here I have received countless greetings from friends who were pleased at my arrival, and from unknown and indeed uninvolved strangers who only wanted to give expression to their satisfaction at my having found freedom and safety here. And in addition there arrived, with a frequency surprising to a foreigner, communications of another sort, which were concerned with the state of my soul, which pointed out to me the way of Christ and sought to enlighten me on the future of Israel. The good people who wrote in this way cannot have known much about me; but I expect that when this work about Moses becomes known, in a translation, among my new compatriots, I shall forfeit enough of the sympathy which a number of other people as well now feel for me.

As regards *internal* difficulties, a political revolution and a change of domicile could alter nothing. No less than before, I feel uncertain in the face of my own work; I lack the consciousness of unity and of belonging together which should exist between an author and his work. It is not as though there were an absence of conviction in the correctness of my conclusion. I acquired that a quarter of a century ago when in 1912 I wrote my book about *Totem and Taboo*, and it has only grown firmer since. From that time I have never doubted that religious phenomena are only to be understood on the pattern of the individual neurotic symptoms familiar to us—as the return of long since forgotten, important events in the primaeval history of the human family—and that they have to thank precisely this origin for their compulsive character and that, accordingly, they are effective on human beings by force of the *historical* truth[1] of their content. My uncertainty sets in only when I ask myself whether I have succeeded in proving these theses in the example which I have chosen here of Jewish monotheism. To my critical sense this book, which takes its start from the man Moses, appears like a dancer balancing on the tip of one toe. If I could not find support in an analytic interpretation of the exposure myth and could not pass from there to Sellin's suspicion about the end of Moses, the whole thing would have had to remain unwritten. In any case, let us now take the plunge.

[1] [See below, p. 127 ff.]

A

The Historical Premiss[1]

Here, then, is the historical background of the events which have absorbed our interest. As a result of the conquests of the Eighteenth Dynasty, Egypt became a world-empire. The new imperialism was reflected in the development of the religious ideas, if not of the whole people, at least of its ruling and intellectually active upper stratum. Under the influence of the priests of the sun-god at On (Heliopolis), strengthened perhaps by impulses from Asia, the idea arose of a universal god Aten to whom restriction to a single country and a single people no longer applied. In the young Amenophis IV a Pharaoh came to the throne who had no higher interest than the development of this idea of a god. He promoted the religion of Aten into the state religion, and through him the universal god became the *only* god: everything that was told of other gods was deceit and lies. With magnificent inflexibility he resisted every temptation to magical thought, and he rejected the illusion, so dear to Egyptians in particular, of a life after death. In an astonishing presentiment of later scientific discovery he recognized in the energy of solar radiation the source of all life on earth and worshipped it as the symbol of the power of his god. He boasted of his joy in the creation and of his life in Ma'at (truth and justice).

This is the first and perhaps the clearest case of a monotheist religion in human history; a deeper insight into the historical and psychological determinants of its origin would be of immeasurable value. Care has however been taken that none too much information about the Aten religion should reach us. Already under Akhenaten's feeble successors all that he had created collapsed. The vengeance of the priesthood which he had suppressed raged against his memory; the Aten religion was abolished, the capital city of the Pharaoh, who was branded as a criminal, was destroyed and plundered. In about 1350 B.C.

[1] I begin with a *résumé* of the findings of my second study on Moses, the purely historical one. Those findings will not be submitted here to any fresh criticism, since they form the premiss to the psychological discussions which start out from them and constantly go back to them.

the Eighteenth Dynasty came to an end; after a period of anarchy, order was restored by general Haremhab, who reigned till 1315 B.C. Akhenaten's reform seemed to be an episode doomed to be forgotten.

Thus far what is established historically; and now our hypothetical sequel begins. Among those in Akhenaten's *entourage* there was a man who was perhaps called Tuthmosis, like many other people at that time[1]—the name is not of great importance except that its second component must have been '—mose'. He was in a high position and a convinced adherent of the Aten religion, but, in contrast to the meditative king, he was energetic and passionate. For him the death of Akhenaten and the abolition of his religion meant the end of all his expectations. He could remain in Egypt only as an outlaw or as a renegade. Perhaps as governor of the frontier province he had come in contact with a Semitic tribe which had immigrated into it a few generations earlier. Under the necessity of his disappointment and loneliness he turned to these foreigners and with them sought compensation for his losses. He chose them as his people and tried to realize his ideals in them. After he had left Egypt with them, accompanied by his followers, he made them holy by the mark of circumcision, gave them laws and introduced them into the doctrines of the Aten religion, which the Egyptians had just thrown off. The precepts which this man Moses gave to his Jews may have been even harsher than those of his master and teacher Akhenaten, and he may, too, have given up dependence on the sun-god of On, to which Akhenaten had continued to adhere.

We must take the period of the interregnum after 1350 B.C. as the date of the Exodus from Egypt. The interval of time which followed, up to the completion of the occupation of the land of Canaan, is particularly inscrutable. Modern historical research has been able to extract two facts from the obscurity which the biblical narrative has left, or rather created, at this point. The first of these facts, discovered by Ernst Sellin, is that the Jews, who, even by the account in the Bible, were headstrong and unruly towards their law-giver and leader, rose against him one day, killed him and threw off the religion of the

[1] Such as, for instance, the sculptor whose studio was found at Tell el-'Amarna.

Aten which had been imposed on them, just as the Egyptians had thrown it off earlier. The second fact, demonstrated by Eduard Meyer, is that those Jews who had returned from Egypt united later on with closely related tribes in the region between Palestine, the Sinai Peninsula and Arabia, and that there, in a well-watered locality named Kadesh, under the influence of the Arabian Midianites, they took on a new religion, the worship of the volcano god Yahweh. Soon after this they were ready to invade Canaan as conquerors.

The chronological relations of these two events to each other and to the Exodus from Egypt are very uncertain. The closest historical point of reference is provided by a stela of the Pharaoh Merenptah (who reigned till 1215 B.C.) which in the course of a report on campaigns in Syria and Palestine names 'Israel' among the defeated enemy. If we take the date of this stela as a *terminus ad quem*, we are left with about a century (from after 1350 to before 1215 B.C.) for the whole course of events, starting from the Exodus. It is possible, however, that the name 'Israel' did not yet relate to the tribes whose fortunes we are following and that in fact we have a longer interval at our disposal. The settlement in Canaan of what was later the Jewish people was certainly no rapidly completed conquest but took place in waves and over considerable periods of time. If we free ourselves from the limitation imposed by the Merenptah stela, we can all the more easily assign one generation (thirty years) to the period of Moses,[1] and allow at least two generations, but probably more, to elapse up to the time of the union at Kadesh.[2] The interval between Kadesh and the irruption into Canaan need only be short. The Jewish tradition, as was shown in the preceding essay [p. 48], had good grounds for shortening the interval between the Exodus and the founding of the religion at Kadesh, while the reverse is in the interest of our account.

All this, however, is still history, an attempt to fill up the gaps in our historical knowledge and in part a repetition of my second essay in *Imago* [Essay II above]. Our interest follows the fortunes of Moses and of his doctrines, to which the rising of the

[1] This would correspond to the forty years of wandering in the wilderness of the Bible text [*Numbers*, xiv, 33].

[2] Thus we should have about 1350 (or 1340)–1320 (or 1310) B.C. for the Moses period; 1260 B.C., or preferably later, for Kadesh; the Merenptah stela before 1215 B.C.

Jews had only apparently put an end. From the account given by the Yahwist, which was written down in about 1000 B.C. but was certainly based on earlier records,[1] we have discovered that the union and the founding of the religion at Kadesh were accompanied by a compromise in which the two sides are still easily distinguishable. The one partner was only concerned to disavow the novelty and foreign character of the god Yahweh and to increase his claim to the people's devotion; the other partner was anxious not to sacrifice to him precious memories of the liberation from Egypt and of the grand figure of the leader, Moses. The second side succeeded, too, in introducing both the fact and the man into the new account of prehistory, in retaining at least the external mark of the religion of Moses—circumcision—and possibly in establishing certain restrictions on the use of the name of the new god. As we have said, the representatives of these claims were the descendants of the followers of Moses, the Levites, who were separated from his contemporaries and compatriots by only a few generations and were still attached to his memory by a living recollection. The poetically embellished narrative which we attribute to the Yahwist, and to his later rival the Elohist, were like mausoleums beneath which, withdrawn from the knowledge of later generations, the true account of those early things—of the nature of the Mosaic religion and of the violent end of the great man—was, as it were, to find its eternal rest. And if we have guessed what happened correctly, there is nothing left about it that is puzzling; but it might very well have signified the final end of the Moses episode in the history of the Jewish people.

The remarkable thing, however, is that that was not the case—that the most powerful effects of the people's experience were to come to light only later and to force their way into reality in the course of many centuries. It is unlikely that Yahweh differed much in character from the gods of the surrounding peoples and tribes. It is true that he struggled with them, just as the peoples themselves fought with one another, but we cannot suppose that it came into the head of a Yahweh-worshipper of those days to deny the existence of the gods of Canaan or

[1] ['*Fixierungen.*' The word is not used here in the usual psycho-analytic sense of 'fixations'. See however, a footnote to Chapter IV of *An Outline of Psycho-Analysis* (1940*a* [1938]), *Standard Ed.*, **23,** 160.]

Moab or Amalek, and so on, any more than to deny the existence of the peoples who believed in them.

The monotheist idea, which had flared up with Akhenaten, had grown dark once more and was to remain in darkness for a long time to come. Finds in the island of Elephantine, just below the First Cataract of the Nile, have given us the surprising information that a Jewish military colony had been settled there for centuries, in whose temple, alongside of the chief god Yahu, two female deities were worshipped, one of them named Anat-Yahu. These Jews, it is true, were cut off from their mother-country and had not taken part in the religious development there; the Persian government of Egypt (of the fifth century B.C.) conveyed information to them of the new rules of worship issued from Jerusalem.[1] Going back to earlier times, we may say that the god Yahweh certainly bore no resemblance to the Mosaic god. Aten had been a pacifist like his representative on earth—or more properly, his prototype—the Pharaoh Akhenaten, who looked on passively while the world-empire conquered by his ancestors fell to pieces. No doubt Yahweh was better suited to a people who were starting out to occupy new homelands by force. And everything in the Mosaic god that deserved admiration was quite beyond the comprehension of the primitive masses.

I have already said—and on that point I have been glad to be able to claim agreement with other writers—that the central fact of the development of the Jewish religion was that in the course of time the god Yahweh lost his own characteristics and grew more and more to resemble the old god of Moses, the Aten. It is true that differences remained to which one would be inclined at a first glance to attribute great importance; but these can easily be explained.

In Egypt Aten had begun to dominate during a fortunate period of established possession, and even when the empire began to totter, his worshippers had been able to turn away from the disturbance and continued to praise and to enjoy his creations. The Jewish people were fated to experience a series of grave trials and painful events; their god became harsh and severe and, as it were, wrapped in gloom. He retained the characteristic of being a universal god, reigning over all countries and peoples, but the fact that his worship had passed over

[1] Auerbach, **2**, 1936.

from the Egyptians to the Jews found expression in the additional belief that the Jews were his chosen people whose special obligations would eventually meet with a special reward as well. It may not have been easy for the people to reconcile a belief in being preferred by their omnipotent god with the sad experiences of their unfortunate destiny. But they did not allow themselves to be shaken in their convictions; they increased their own sense of guilt in order to stifle their doubts of God, and it may be that they pointed at last to the 'inscrutable decrees of Providence', as pious people do to this day. If they felt inclined to wonder at his allowing one violent aggressor after another to arise and overthrow and maltreat them—Assyrians, Babylonians, Persians—they could yet recognize his power in the fact that all these evil foes were themselves conquered in turn and that their empires vanished.

In three important respects the later god of the Jews became in the end like the old Mosaic god. The first and decisive point is that he was truly acknowledged as the only god, beside whom any other god was unthinkable. Akhenaten's monotheism was taken seriously by an entire people; indeed, that people clung so much to this idea that it became the main content of their intellectual life[1] and left them no interest for other things. On this the people and the priesthood who had become dominant among them were at one. But whereas the priests exhausted their efforts in erecting the ceremonial for his worship, they came in opposition to intense currents among the people which sought to revive two others of the doctrines of Moses about his god. The voices of the Prophets never tired of declaring that God despised ceremonial and sacrifice and required only that people should believe in him and lead a life in truth and justice. And when they praised the simplicity and holiness of life in the wilderness they were certainly under the influence of the Mosaic ideals.

It is time to raise the question of whether there is any need whatever to call in the influence of Moses as a cause of the final form taken by the Jewish idea of God, or whether it would not be enough to assume a spontaneous development to higher intellectuality[2] during a cultural life extending over hundreds

[1] ['*Geistesleben.*' Cf. the next footnote.]

[2] ['*Geistigkeit.*' See the discussion of the rendering of this word in the footnote on p. 86 below.]

of years. There are two things to be said about this possible explanation which would put an end to all our puzzling conjectures. First, that it explains nothing. In the case of the Greeks—unquestionably a most highly gifted people—the same conditions did not lead to monotheism but to a disintegration of their polytheist religion and to the beginning of philosophical thought. In Egypt, so far as we can understand, monotheism grew up as a by-product of imperialism: God was a reflection of the Pharaoh who was the absolute ruler of a great world-empire. With the Jews, political conditions were highly unfavourable for the development from the idea of an exclusive national god to that of a universal ruler of the world. And where did this tiny and powerless nation find the arrogance to declare itself the favourite child of the great Lord? The problem of the origin of monotheism among the Jews would thus remain unsolved, or we should have to be content with the common answer that it is the expression of the peculiar religious genius of that people. Genius is well known to be incomprehensible and irresponsible, and we ought therefore not to bring it up as an explanation till every other solution has failed us.[1]

In addition to this, we come upon the fact that Jewish records and historical writings themselves point us the way, by asserting most definitely—this time without contradicting themselves—that the idea of a single god was brought to the people by Moses. If there is an objection to the trustworthiness of this assurance, it is that the priestly revision of the text we have before us obviously traces far too much back to Moses. Institutions such as the ritual ordinances, which date unmistakably from later times, are given out as Mosaic commandments with the plain intention of lending them authority. This certainly gives us ground for suspicion, but not enough for a rejection. For the deeper motive for an exaggeration of this kind is obvious. The priestly narrative seeks to establish continuity between its contemporary period and the remote Mosaic past; it seeks to disavow precisely what we have described as the most striking fact about Jewish religious history, namely that there is a yawning gap between the law-giving of Moses and the later Jewish religion—a gap which was at first filled by the worship

[1] This same consideration applies, too, to the remarkable case of William Shakespeare of Stratford. [See footnote to *An Outline of Psycho-Analysis*, *Standard Ed.*, **23**, 192.]

of Yahweh, and was only slowly patched up afterwards. It disputes this course of events by every possible means, though its historical correctness is established beyond any doubt, since, in the particular treatment given to the Biblical text, superabundant evidence has been left to prove it. Here the priestly revision has attempted something similar to the tendentious distortion which made the new god Yahweh into the god of the Patriarchs [p. 44]. If we take this motive of the Priestly Code into account, we shall find it hard to withhold our belief from the assertion that Moses really did himself give the monotheist idea to the Jews. We should be all the readier to give our assent since we can say where Moses derived this idea from, which the Jewish priests certainly knew no longer.

And here someone might ask what we gain by tracing Jewish to Egyptian monotheism. It merely pushes the problem a little way further back: it tells us nothing more of the genesis of the monotheist idea. The answer is that the question is not one of gain but of investigation. Perhaps we may learn something from it if we discover the real course of events.

B

The Latency Period and Tradition

We confess the belief, therefore, that the idea of a single god, as well as the rejection of magically effective ceremonial and the stress upon ethical demands made in his name, were in fact Mosaic doctrines, to which no attention was paid to begin with, but which, after a long interval had elapsed, came into operation and eventually became permanently established. How are we to explain a delayed effect of this kind and where do we meet with a similar phenomenon?

It occurs to us at once that such things are not infrequently to be found in the most various spheres and that they probably come about in a number of ways which are understandable with greater or less ease. Let us take, for instance, the history of a new scientific theory, such as Darwin's theory of evolution. At first it met with embittered rejection and was violently disputed for decades; but it took no longer than a generation for it to be recognized as a great step forward towards truth. Darwin himself achieved the honour of a grave or cenotaph in Westminster Abbey. A case such as that leaves us little to unravel. The new truth awoke emotional resistances; these found expression in arguments by which the evidence in favour of the unpopular theory could be disputed; the struggle of opinions took up a certain length of time; from the first there were adherents and opponents; the number as well as the weight of the former kept on increasing till at last they gained the upper hand; during the whole time of the struggle the subject with which it was concerned was never forgotten. We are scarcely surprised that the whole course of events took a considerable length of time; and we probably do not sufficiently appreciate that what we are concerned with is a process in group psychology.

There is no difficulty in finding an analogy in the mental life of an individual corresponding precisely to this process. Such would be the case if a person learnt something new to him which, on the ground of certain evidence, he ought to recognize as true, but which contradicts some of his wishes and shocks a few convictions that are precious to him. Thereupon he will hesitate, seek for reasons to enable him to throw doubts on this new thing, and for a while will struggle with himself, till finally he admits to himself: 'All the same it *is* so, though it's not easy for me to accept it, though it's distressing to me to have to believe it.' What we learn from this is merely that it takes time for the reasoning activity of the ego to overcome the objections that are maintained by strong affective cathexes. The similarity between this case and the one we are endeavouring to understand is not very great.

The next example we turn to appears to have even less in common with our problem. It may happen that a man who has experienced some frightful accident—a railway collision, for instance—leaves the scene of the event apparently uninjured. In the course of the next few weeks, however, he develops a number of severe psychical and motor symptoms which can only be traced to his shock, the concussion or whatever else it was. He now has a 'traumatic neurosis'. It is a quite unintelligible —that is to say, a new—fact. The time that has passed between the accident and the first appearance of the symptoms is described as the 'incubation period', in a clear allusion to the pathology of infectious diseases. On reflection, it must strike us that, in spite of the fundamental difference between the two cases—the problem of traumatic neurosis and that of Jewish monotheism—there is nevertheless one point of agreement: namely, in the characteristic that might be described as 'latency'. According to our assured hypothesis, in the history of the Jewish religion there was a long period after the defection from the religion of Moses during which no sign was to be detected of the monotheist idea, of the contempt for ceremonial or of the great emphasis on ethics. We are thus prepared for the possibility that the solution of our problem is to be looked for in a particular psychological situation.

We have already repeatedly described what happened at Kadesh when the two portions of what was later to be the Jewish people came together to receive a new religion. In those, on the one hand, who had been in Egypt, memories of the Exodus and of the figure of Moses were still so strong and vivid that they demanded their inclusion in an account of early times. They were grandchildren, perhaps, of people who had known Moses himself, and some of them still felt themselves Egyptians and bore Egyptian names. But they had good motives for repressing the memory of the fate with which their leader and lawgiver had met. The determining purpose of the other portion of the people was to glorify the new god and to dispute his being foreign. Both portions had the same interest in disavowing the fact of their having had an earlier religion and the nature of its content. So it was that the first compromise came about, and it was probably soon recorded in writing. The people who had come from Egypt had brought writing and the desire to write history along with them; but it was to be a long time before historical writing realized that it was pledged to unswerving truthfulness. To begin with it had no scruples about shaping its narratives according to the needs and purposes of the moment, as though it had not yet recognized the concept of falsification. As a result of these circumstances a discrepancy was able to grow up between the written record and the oral transmission of the same material—*tradition*. What had been omitted or changed in the written record might very well have been preserved intact in tradition. Tradition was a supplement but at the same time a contradiction to historical writing. It was less subjected to the influence of distorting purposes and perhaps at some points quite exempt from them, and it might therefore be more truthful than the account that had been recorded in writing. Its trustworthiness, however, suffered from the fact that it was less stable and definite than the written account and exposed to numerous changes and alterations when it was handed on from one generation to another by oral communication. A tradition of such a kind might meet with various sorts of fate. What we should most expect would be that it would be crushed by the written account, would be unable to stand up against it, would become more and more shadowy and would finally pass into oblivion. But it might meet with other fates: one of these would be that the tradition itself would end in a written record, and we shall have to deal with yet others as we proceed.

The phenomenon of latency in the history of the Jewish religion, with which we are dealing, may be explained, then, by the circumstance that the facts and ideas which were intentionally disavowed by what may be called the official historians were in fact never lost. Information about them persisted in traditions which survived among the people. As we are assured by Sellin, indeed, there was actually a tradition about the end of Moses which flatly contradicted the official account and was far nearer the truth. The same, we may assume, also applied to other things which apparently ceased to exist at the same time as Moses—to some of the contents of the Mosaic religion, which had been unacceptable to the majority of his contemporaries.

The remarkable fact with which we are here confronted is, however, that these traditions, instead of becoming weaker with time, became more and more powerful in the course of centuries, forced their way into the later revisions of the official accounts and finally showed themselves strong enough to have a decisive influence on the thoughts and actions of the people. The determinants which made this outcome possible are for the moment, it is true, outside our knowledge.

This fact is so remarkable that we feel justified in looking at it once again. Our problem is comprised in it. The Jewish people had abandoned the Aten religion brought to them by Moses and had turned to the worship of another god who differed little from the Baalim[1] of the neighbouring peoples.

[1] [Local gods.]

All the tendentious efforts of later times failed to disguise this shameful fact. But the Mosaic religion had not vanished without leaving a trace; some sort of memory of it had kept alive—a possibly obscured and distorted tradition. And it was this tradition of a great past which continued to operate (from the background, as it were), which gradually acquired more and more power over people's minds and which in the end succeeded in changing the god Yahweh into the Mosaic god and in re-awakening into life the religion of Moses that had been introduced and then abandoned long centuries before. That a tradition thus sunk in oblivion should exercise such a powerful effect on the mental life of a people is an unfamiliar idea to us. We find ourselves here in the field of group psychology, where we do not feel at home. We shall look about for analogies, for facts that are at least of a similar nature, even though in different fields. And facts of that sort are, I believe, to be found.

During the period at which, among the Jews, the return of the religion of Moses was in preparation, the Greek people found themselves in possession of an exceedingly rich store of tribal legends and hero-myths. It is believed that the ninth or eighth century B.C. saw the origin of the two Homeric epics, which drew their material from this circle of legends. With our present psychological insight we could, long before Schliemann and Evans, have raised the question of where it was that the Greeks obtained all the legendary material which was worked over by Homer and the great Attic dramatists in their masterpieces. The answer would have had to be that this people had probably experienced in their prehistory a period of external brilliance and cultural efflorescence which had perished in a historical catastrophe and of which an obscure tradition survived in these legends. The archaeological researches of our days have now confirmed this suspicion, which in the past would certainly have been pronounced too daring. These researches have uncovered the evidences of the impressive Minoan–Mycenaean civilization, which had probably already come to an end on the mainland of Greece before 1250 B.C. There is scarcely a hint at it to be found in the Greek historians of a later age: at most a remark that there was a time when the Cretans exercised command of the sea, and the name of King Minos and of his palace, the Labyrinth. That is all, and beyond it nothing has remained but the traditions which were seized on by the poets.

National epics of other peoples—Germans, Indians, Finns—have come to light as well. It is the business of historians of literature to investigate whether we may assume the same determinants for their origin as with the Greeks. Such an investigation would, I believe, yield a positive result. Here is the determinant which we recognize: a piece of prehistory which, immediately after it, would have been bound to appear rich in content, important, splendid, and always, perhaps, heroic, but which lies so far back, in such remote times, that only an obscure and incomplete tradition informs later generations of it. Surprise has been felt that the epic as an art-form has become extinct in later times. The explanation may be that its determining cause no longer exists. The old material was used up and for all later events historical writing took the place of tradition. The greatest heroic deeds of our days have not been able to inspire an epic, and even Alexander the Great had a right to complain that he would find no Homer.

Long-past ages have a great and often puzzling attraction for men's imagination. Whenever they are dissatisfied with their present surroundings—and this happens often enough—they turn back to the past and hope that they will now be able to prove the truth of the unextinguishable dream of a golden age.[1] They are probably still under the spell of their childhood, which is presented to them by their not impartial memory as a time of uninterrupted bliss.

If all that is left of the past are the incomplete and blurred memories which we call tradition, this offers an artist a peculiar attraction, for in that case he is free to fill in the gaps in memory according to the desires of his imagination and to picture the period which he wishes to reproduce according to his intentions. One might almost say that the vaguer a tradition has become the more serviceable it becomes for a poet. We need not therefore be surprised at the importance of tradition for imaginative writing, and the analogy with the manner in which epics are determined will make us more inclined to accept the strange

[1] This was the situation on which Macaulay based his *Lays of Ancient Rome*. He put himself in the place of a minstrel who, depressed by the confused party strife of his own day, presented his hearers with the self-sacrifice, the unity and the patriotism of their ancestors.

hypothesis that it was the tradition of Moses which, for the Jews, altered the worship of Yahweh in the direction of the old Mosaic religion. But in other respects the two cases are still too different. On the one hand the outcome is a poem and on the other a religion; and in the latter instance we have assumed that, under the spur of tradition, it was reproduced with a faithfulness for which the instance of the epic can of course offer no counterpart. Accordingly enough of our problem is left over to justify a need for more apposite analogies.

C

The Analogy

The only satisfying analogy to the remarkable course of events that we have found in the history of the Jewish religion lies in an apparently remote field; but it is very complete, and approaches identity. In it we once more come upon the phenomenon of latency, the emergence of unintelligible manifestations calling for an explanation and an early, and later forgotten, event as a necessary determinant. We also find the characteristic of compulsion, which forces itself on the mind along with an overpowering of logical thought—a feature which did not come into account, for instance, in the genesis of the epic.

This analogy is met with in psychopathology, in the genesis of human neuroses—in a field, that is to say, belonging to the psychology of individuals, while religious phenomena have of course to be reckoned as part of group psychology. We shall see that this analogy is not so surprising as might at first be thought—indeed that it is more like a postulate.

We give the name of *traumas* to those impressions, experienced early and later forgotten, to which we attach such great importance in the aetiology of the neuroses. We may leave on one side the question of whether the aetiology of the neuroses in general may be regarded as traumatic. The obvious objection to this is that it is not possible in every case to discover a manifest trauma in the neurotic subject's earliest history. We must often resign ourselves to saying that all we have before us is an unusual, abnormal reaction to experiences and demands which affect everyone, but are worked over and dealt with by other people in another manner which may be called normal. When we have nothing else at our disposal for explaining a neurosis but hereditary and constitutional dispositions, we are naturally tempted to say that it was not acquired but developed.

But in this connection two points must be stressed. Firstly, the genesis of a neurosis invariably goes back to very early impressions in childhood.[1] Secondly, it is true that there are cases which are distinguished as being 'traumatic' because their effects go back unmistakably to one or more powerful impressions in these early times—impressions which have escaped being dealt with normally, so that one is inclined to judge that if they had not occurred the neurosis would not have come about either. It would be enough for our purposes if we were obliged to restrict the analogy we are in search of to these traumatic cases. But the gap between the two groups [of cases] appears not to be unbridgeable. It is quite possible to unite the two aetiological determinants under a single conception; it is merely a question of how one defines 'traumatic'. If we may assume that the experience acquires its traumatic character only as a result of a quantitative factor—that is to say, that in every case it is an excess in demand that is responsible for an experience evoking unusual pathological reactions—then we can easily arrive at the expedient of saying that something acts as a trauma in the case of one constitution but in the case of another would have no such effect. In this way we reach the concept of a sliding 'complemental series' as it is called,[2] in which two factors converge in fulfilling an aetiological requirement. A less of one factor is balanced by a more of the other; as a rule both factors operate together and it is only at the two ends of the series that there can be any question of a simple motive being at work. After mentioning this, we can disregard the distinction between traumatic and non-traumatic aetiologies as irrelevant to the analogy we are in search of.

In spite of a risk of repetition, it will perhaps be as well to bring together here the facts which comprise the analogy that is

[1] This therefore makes it nonsensical to say that one is practising psycho-analysis if one excludes from examination and consideration precisely these earliest periods—as happens in some quarters. [Cf. Freud's criticisms of Jung's views in his 'History of the Psycho-Analytic Movement' (1914*d*), particularly in *Standard Ed.*, **14,** 63.]

[2] [See *Introductory Lectures*, XXII, (1916–17), *Standard Ed.*, **16,** 347.]

significant for us. They are as follows. Our researches have shown that what we call the phenomena (symptoms) of a neurosis are the result of certain experiences and impressions which for that very reason we regard as aetiological traumas. We now have two tasks before us: to discover (1) the common characteristics of these experiences and (2) those of neurotic symptoms, and in doing so we need not avoid drawing a somewhat schematic picture.

(1) (*a*) All these traumas occur in early childhood up to about the fifth year. Impressions from the time at which a child is beginning to talk stand out as being of particular interest; the periods between the ages of two and four seem to be the most important; it cannot be determined with certainty how long after birth this period of receptivity begins. (*b*) The experiences in question are as a rule totally forgotten, they are not accessible to memory and fall within the period of infantile amnesia, which is usually broken into by a few separate mnemic residues, what are known as 'screen memories'.[1] (*c*) They relate to impressions of a sexual and aggressive nature, and no doubt also to early injuries to the ego (narcissistic mortifications). In this connection it should be remarked that such young children make no sharp distinction between sexual and aggressive acts, as they do later. (Cf. the misunderstanding of the sexual act in a sadistic sense.[2]) The predominance of the sexual factor is, of course, most striking and calls for theoretical consideration.

These three points—the very early appearance of these experiences (during the first five years of life), the fact of their being forgotten and their sexual-aggressive content—are closely interconnected. The traumas are either experiences on the subject's own body or sense perceptions, mostly of something seen and heard—that is, experiences or impressions. The interconnection of these three points is established by a theory, a product of the work of analysis which alone can bring about a knowledge of the forgotten experiences, or, to put it more vividly but also more incorrectly, bring them back to memory. The theory is that, in contrast to popular opinion, the sexual life of human beings (or what corresponds to it later on) exhibits an early efflorescence which comes to an end at about

[1] [See *Introductory Lectures*, XIII, (1916–17), ibid., **15**, 200–1.]

[2] ['The Sexual Theories of Children' (1908*c*), *Standard Ed.*, **9**, 220–2.]

the fifth year and is followed by what is known as the period of latency (till puberty) in which there is no further development of sexuality and indeed what has been attained undergoes a retrogression. This theory is confirmed by the anatomical investigation of the growth of the internal genitalia; it leads us to suppose that the human race is descended from a species of animal which reached sexual maturity in five years and rouses a suspicion that the postponement of sexual life and its diphasic onset [in two waves] are intimately connected with the history of hominization.[1] Human beings appear to be the only animal organisms with a latency period and sexual retardation of this kind. Investigations on the primates (which, so far as I know, are not available) would be indispensable for testing this theory. It cannot be a matter of indifference psychologically that the period of infantile amnesia coincides with this early period of sexuality. It may be that this state of things provides the true determinant for the possibility of neurosis, which is in a sense a human prerogative and from this point of view appears as a vestige—a 'survival' [2]—of primaeval times like certain portions of our bodily anatomy.

(2) Two points must be stressed in regard to the common characteristics or peculiarities of neurotic phenomena: (*a*) The effects of traumas are of two kinds, positive and negative. The former are attempts to bring the trauma into operation once again—that is, to remember the forgotten experience or, better still, to make it real, to experience a repetition of it anew, or, even if it was only an early emotional relationship, to revive it in an analogous relationship with someone else. We summarize these efforts under the name of 'fixations' to the trauma and as a 'compulsion to repeat'. They may be taken up into what passes as a normal ego and, as permanent trends in it, may lend it unalterable character-traits, although, or rather precisely because, their true basis and historical origin are forgotten. Thus a man who has spent his childhood in an excessive and to-day forgotten attachment to his mother, may spend his whole life looking for a wife on whom he can make himself dependent and by whom he can arrange to be nourished and supported. A girl who was made the object of a sexual seduction in her early

[1] ['*Menschwerdung*', 'the process of becoming human'.]
[2] [In English in the original.]

childhood may direct her later sexual life so as constantly to provoke similar attacks. It may easily be guessed that from such discoveries about the problem of neurosis we can penetrate to an understanding of the formation of character in general.

The negative reactions follow the opposite aim: that nothing of the forgotten traumas shall be remembered and nothing repeated. We can summarize them as 'defensive reactions'. Their principal expression are what are called 'avoidances', which may be intensified into 'inhibitions' and 'phobias'. These negative reactions too make the most powerful contributions to the stamping of character. Fundamentally they are just as much fixations to the trauma as their opposites, except that they are fixations with a contrary purpose. The symptoms of neurosis in the narrower sense are compromises in which both the trends proceeding from traumas come together, so that the share, now of one and now of the other tendency, finds preponderant expression in them. This opposition between the reactions sets up conflicts which in the ordinary course of events can reach no conclusion.

(*b*) All these phenomena, the symptoms as well as the restrictions on the ego and the stable character-changes, have a *compulsive* quality: that is to say that they have great psychical intensity and at the same time exhibit a far-reaching independence of the organization of the other mental processes, which are adjusted to the demands of the real external world and obey the laws of logical thinking. They [the pathological phenomena] are insufficiently or not at all influenced by external reality, pay no attention to it or to its psychical representatives, so that they may easily come into active opposition to both of them. They are, one might say, a State within a State, an inaccessible party, with which co-operation is impossible, but which may succeed in overcoming what is known as the normal party and forcing it into its service. If this happens, it implies a domination by an internal psychical reality over the reality of the external world and the path to a psychosis lies open.[1] Even if things do not go so far, the

[1] [The distinction between psychical and external reality was already made in Section 2 of Part III of the *Project* of 1895 (1950*a*, *Standard Ed.*, **1**), where a discussion of Freud's use of the terms will be found in an Editor's footnote.—Cf. also p. 130 *n.* below]

practical importance of this situation can scarcely be overestimated. The inhibition upon the life of those who are dominated by a neurosis and their incapacity for living constitute a most important factor in a human society and we may recognize in their condition a direct expression of their fixation to an early portion of their past.

And now let us enquire about latency, which, in view of the analogy, is bound to interest us especially. A trauma in childhood may be followed immediately by a neurotic outbreak, an infantile neurosis, with an abundance of efforts at defence, and accompanied by the formation of symptoms. This neurosis may last a considerable time and cause marked disturbances, but it may also run a latent course and be overlooked. As a rule defence retains the upper hand in it; in any case alterations of the ego,[1] comparable to scars, are left behind. It is only rarely that an infantile neurosis continues without interruption into an adult one. Far more often it is succeeded by a period of apparently undisturbed development—a course of things which is supported or made possible by the intervention of the physiological period of latency. Not until later does the change take place with which the definitive neurosis becomes manifest as a belated effect of the trauma. This occurs either at the irruption of puberty or some while later. In the former case it happens because the instincts, intensified by physical maturation, are able now to take up the struggle again in which they were at first defeated by the defence. In the latter case it happens because the reactions and alterations of the ego brought about by the defence now prove a hindrance in dealing with the new tasks of life, so that severe conflicts come about between the demands of the real external world and the ego, which seeks to maintain the organization which it has painstakingly achieved in its defensive struggle. The phenomenon of a latency of the neurosis between the first reactions to the trauma and the later outbreak of the illness must be regarded as typical. This latter illness may also be looked upon as an attempt at cure—as an effort once more to reconcile with the rest those portions of the ego that have been split off by the influence of the trauma and to unite them into a powerful

[1] [See a discussion in the Editor's Note to 'Analysis Terminable and Interminable' (1937*c*), *S.E.*, **23,** 212–13, and Section V of that paper.]

whole *vis-à-vis* the external world. An attempt of this kind seldom succeeds, however, unless the work of analysis comes to its help, and even then not always; it ends often enough in a complete devastation or fragmentation of the ego or in its being overwhelmed[1] by the portion which was early split off and which is dominated by the trauma.

In order to convince the reader, it would be necessary to give detailed reports of the life histories of numerous neurotics. But in view of the diffuseness and difficulty of the topic, this would completely destroy the character of the present work. It would turn into a monograph on the theory of the neuroses and even so would probably only have an effect on that minority of readers who have chosen the study and practice of psycho-analysis as their life-work. Since I am addressing myself here to a wider audience, I can only beg the reader to grant a certain provisional credence to the abridged account I have given above; and this must be accompanied by an admission on my part that the implications to which I am now leading him need only be accepted if the theories on which they are based turn out to be correct.

Nevertheless, I can attempt to tell the story of a single case which exhibits with special clarity some of the characteristics of a neurosis which I have mentioned. We must not expect, of course, that a single case will show everything and we need not feel disappointed if its subject-matter is far removed from the topic for which we are seeking an analogy.

A little boy, who, as is so often the case in middle-class families, shared his parents' bedroom during the first years of his life, had repeated, and indeed regular, opportunities of observing sexual acts between his parents—of seeing some things and hearing still more—at an age when he had scarcely learnt to speak. In his later neurosis, which broke out immediately after his first spontaneous emission, the earliest and most troublesome symptom was a disturbance of sleep. He was extraordinarily sensitive to noises at night and, once he was woken up, was unable to go to sleep again. This disturbance of sleep was a true compromise-symptom. On the one hand it was an

[1] [Cf. an Editor's footnote to *The Ego and the Id* (1923*b*), *Standard Ed.*, **19**, 57, and another to Draft K (1950*a*), ibid., **1**, 222–3 *n.*]

expression of his defence against the things he had experienced at night, and on the other an attempt to re-establish the waking state in which he was able to listen to those impressions.

The child was aroused prematurely by observations of this kind to an aggressive masculinity and began to excite his little penis with his hand and to attempt various sexual attacks on his mother, thus identifying himself with his father, in whose place he was putting himself. This went on until at last his mother forbade him to touch his penis and further threatened that she would tell his father, who would punish him by taking his sinful organ away. This threat of castration had an extraordinarily powerful traumatic effect on the boy. He gave up his sexual activity and altered his character. Instead of identifying himself with his father, he was afraid of him, adopted a passive attitude to him and, by occasional naughtinesses, provoked him into administering corporal punishment; this had a sexual meaning for him, so that he was thus able to identify himself with his ill-treated mother. He clung to his mother herself more and more anxiously, as though he could not do without her love for a single moment, since he saw in it a protection against the danger of castration which threatened him from his father. In this modification of the Oedipus complex he passed his latency period, which was free from any marked disturbances. He became an exemplary boy and was quite successful at school.

So far we have followed the immediate effect of the trauma and have confirmed the fact of latency.

The arrival of puberty brought with it the manifest neurosis and disclosed its second main symptom—sexual impotence. He had forfeited the sensitivity of his penis, did not attempt to touch it, did not venture to approach a woman for sexual purposes. His sexual activity remained limited to psychical masturbation accompanied by sadistic-masochistic phantasies in which it was not hard to recognize off-shoots of his early observations of intercourse between his parents. The wave of intensified masculinity which puberty brought along with it was employed in furious hatred of his father and insubordination to him. This extreme relation to his father, reckless to the pitch of self-destruction, was responsible as well for his failure in life and his conflicts with the external world. He must be a failure in his profession because his father had forced him into it. Nor did he make any friends and he was never on good terms with his superiors.

When, burdened by these symptoms and incapacities, he at last, after his father's death, had found a wife, there emerged in him, as though they were the core of his being, character-traits which made contact with him a hard task for those about him. He developed a completely egoistic, despotic, and brutal personality, which clearly felt a need to suppress and insult other people. It was a faithful copy of his father as he had formed a picture of him in his memory: that is to say, a revival of the identification with his father which in the past he had taken on as a little boy from sexual motives. In this part of the story we recognize the *return* of the repressed, which (along with the immediate effects of the trauma and the phenomenon of latency) we have described as among the essential features of a neurosis.

D

Application

Early trauma—defence—latency—outbreak of neurotic illness—partial return of the repressed. Such is the formula which we have laid down for the development of a neurosis. The reader is now invited to take the step of supposing that something occurred in the life of the human species similar to what occurs in the life of individuals: of supposing, that is, that here too events occurred of a sexually aggressive nature, which left behind them permanent consequences but were for the most part fended off and forgotten, and which after a long latency came into effect and created phenomena similar to symptoms in their structure and purpose.

We believe that we can guess these events and we propose to show that their symptom-like consequences are the phenomena of religion. Since the emergence of the idea of evolution no longer leaves room for doubt that the human race has a prehistory, and since this is unknown—that is, forgotten—a conclusion of this kind almost carries the weight of a postulate. When we learn that in both cases the operative and forgotten traumas relate to life in the human family, we can greet this as a highly welcome, unforeseen bonus which has not been called for by our discussions up to this point.

I put forward these assertions as much as a quarter of a century ago in my *Totem and Taboo* (1912–13) and I need only repeat them here. My construction starts out from a statement of Darwin's [1871, **2**, 362 f.] and takes in a hypothesis of Atkinson's [1903, 220 f.]. It asserts that in primaeval times primitive man lived in small hordes,[1] each under the domination of a powerful male. No date can be assigned to this, nor has it been synchronized with the geological epochs known to us: it is probable that these human creatures had not advanced far in the development of speech. An essential part of the construction is the hypothesis that the events I am about to describe occurred to all primitive men—that is, to all our ancestors. The story is told in an enormously condensed form, as though it had happened on a single occasion, while in fact it covered thousands of years and was repeated countless times during that long period. The strong male was lord and father of the entire horde and unrestricted in his power, which he exercised with violence. All the females were his property—wives and daughters of his own horde and some, perhaps, robbed from other hordes. The lot of his sons was a hard one: if they roused their father's jealousy they were killed or castrated or driven out. Their only resource was to collect together in small communities, to get themselves wives by robbery, and, when one or other of them could succeed in it, to raise themselves into a position similar to their father's in the primal horde. For natural reasons, youngest sons occupied an exceptional position. They were protected by their mother's love, and were able to take advantage of their father's increasing age and succeed him on his death. We seem to detect echoes in legends and fairy tales both of the expulsion of elder sons and of the favouring of youngest sons.

The first decisive step towards a change in this sort of 'social' organization seems to have been that the expelled brothers, living in a community, united to overpower their father and, as was the custom in those days, devoured him raw. There is no need to balk at this cannibalism; it continued far into later times. The essential point, however, is that we attribute the

[1] [Freud always uses this term in the sense of a small and more or less organized group. See *Totem and Taboo*, *Standard Ed.*, **13,** 125 *n.* 2.]

same emotional attitudes to these primitive men that we are able to establish by analytic investigation in the primitives of the present day—in our children. We suppose, that is, that they not only hated and feared their father but also honoured him as a model, and that each of them wished to take his place in reality. We can, if so, understand the cannibalistic act as an attempt to ensure identification with him by incorporating a piece of him.

It must be supposed that after the parricide a considerable time elapsed during which the brothers disputed with one another for their father's heritage, which each of them wanted for himself alone. A realization of the dangers and uselessness of these struggles, a recollection of the act of liberation which they had accomplished together, and the emotional ties with one another which had arisen during the period of their expulsion, led at last to an agreement among them, a sort of social contract. The first form of a social organization came about with a *renunciation of instinct*,[1] a recognition of mutual *obligations*, the introduction of definite *institutions*, pronounced inviolable (holy) —that is to say, the beginnings of morality and justice. Each individual renounced his ideal of acquiring his father's position for himself and of possessing his mother and sisters. Thus the *taboo on incest* and the injunction to *exogamy* came about. A fair amount of the absolute power liberated by the removal of the father passed over to the women; there came a period of *matriarchy*. Recollection of their father persisted at this period of the 'fraternal alliance'. A powerful animal—at first, perhaps, always one that was feared as well—was chosen as a substitute for the father. A choice of this kind may seem strange, but the gulf which men established later between themselves and animals did not exist for primitive peoples; nor does it exist for our children, whose animal phobias we have been able to understand as fear of their father. In relation to the totem animal the original dichotomy in the emotional relation to the father (ambivalence) was wholly retained. On the one hand the totem was regarded as the clan's blood ancestor and protective spirit, who must be worshipped and protected, and on the other hand a festival was appointed at which the same fate was prepared for him that the primal father had met with. He was killed and devoured by all the tribesmen in common. (The

[1] [This is the subject of Section D of Part II, p. 116 ff. below.]

totem meal, according to Robertson Smith [1894].) This great festival was in fact a triumphant celebration of the combined sons' victory over their father.

What is the place of religion in this connection? I think we are completely justified in regarding totemism, with its worship of a father-substitute, with its ambivalence as shown by the totem meal, with its institution of memorial festivals and of prohibitions whose infringement was punished by death—we are justified, I say, in regarding totemism as the first form in which religion was manifested in human history and in confirming the fact of its having been linked from the first with social regulations and moral obligations. Here we can only give the most summary survey of the further developments of religion. They no doubt proceeded in parallel with the cultural advances of the human race and with the changes in the structure of human communities.

The first step away from totemism was the humanizing of the being who was worshipped. In place of the animals, human gods appear, whose derivation from the totem is not concealed. The god is still represented either in the form of an animal or at least with an animal's face, or the totem becomes the god's favourite companion, inseparable from him, or legend tells us that the god slew this precise animal, which was after all only a preliminary stage of himself. At a point in this evolution which is not easily determined great mother-goddesses appeared, probably even before the male gods, and afterwards persisted for a long time beside them. In the meantime a great social revolution had occurred. Matriarchy was succeeded by the re-establishment of a patriarchal order. The new fathers, it is true, never achieved the omnipotence of the primal father; there were many of them, who lived together in associations larger than the horde had been. They were obliged to be on good terms with one another, and remained under the limitation of social ordinances. It is likely that the mother-goddesses originated at the time of the curtailment of the matriarchy, as a compensation for the slight upon the mothers. The male deities appear first as sons beside the great mothers and only later clearly assume the features of father-figures. These male gods of polytheism reflect the conditions during the patriarchal age. They are numerous, mutually restrictive, and are occasionally subordinated to a superior high god. The next step, however, leads us to the theme with which we are here concerned—to the return of a single father-god of unlimited dominion.[1]

It must be admitted that this historical survey has gaps in it and is uncertain at some points. But anyone who is inclined to pronounce our construction of primaeval history purely imaginary would be gravely under-estimating the wealth and evidential value of the material contained in it. Large portions of the past, which have been linked together here into a whole, are historically attested: totemism and the male confederacies, for instance. Other portions have survived in excellent replicas. Thus authorities have often been struck by the faithful way in which the sense and content of the old totem meal is repeated in the rite of the Christian Communion, in which the believer incorporates the blood and flesh of his god in symbolic form. Numerous relics of the forgotten primaeval age have survived in popular legends and fairy tales, and the analytic study of the mental life of children has provided an unexpected wealth of material for filling the gaps in our knowledge of the earliest times. As contributions to our understanding of the son's relation to the father which is of such great importance, I need only bring forward animal phobias, the fear, which strikes us as so strange, of being eaten by the father, and the enormous intensity of the dread of being castrated. There is nothing wholly fabricated in our construction, nothing which could not be supported on solid foundations.

If our account of primaeval history is accepted as on the whole worthy of belief, two sorts of elements will be recognized in religious doctrines and rituals: on the one hand fixations to the ancient history of the family and survivals of it, and on the other hand revivals of the past and returns, after long intervals, of what has been forgotten. It is this last portion which, hitherto overlooked and therefore not understood, is to be demonstrated here in at least one impressive instance.

[1] [The greater part of the material in this account will be found discussed at much greater length in the fourth essay of *Totem and Taboo*, though there is rather more discussion here than anywhere else of the mother-goddesses. (On this last point, cf. the footnote on p. 46 above. See also some remarks in Chapter XII of *Group Psychology* (1921*c*), *Standard Ed.*, **18**, 135 and 137.) The general subject is taken up again in Section D of Part II, p. 119 ff. below.]

It is worth specially stressing the fact that each portion which returns from oblivion asserts itself with peculiar force, exercises an incomparably powerful influence on people in the mass, and raises an irresistible claim to truth against which logical objections remain powerless: a kind of '*credo quia absurdum*'.[1] This remarkable feature can only be understood on the pattern of the delusions of psychotics. We have long understood that a portion of forgotten truth lies hidden in delusional ideas, that when this returns it has to put up with distortions and misunderstandings, and that the compulsive conviction which attaches to the delusion arises from this core of truth and spreads out on to the errors that wrap it round. We must grant an ingredient such as this of what may be called *historical* truth to the dogmas of religion as well, which, it is true, bear the character of psychotic symptoms but which, as group phenomena, escape the curse of isolation.[2]

No other portion of the history of religion has become so clear to us as the introduction of monotheism into Judaism and its continuation in Christianity—if we leave on one side the development which we can trace no less uninterruptedly, from the animal totem to the human god with his regular companions. (Each of the four Christian evangelists still has his own favourite animal.) If we provisionally accept the world-empire of the Pharaohs as the determining cause of the emergence of the monotheist idea, we see that that idea, released from its native soil and transferred to another people was, after a long period of latency, taken hold of by them, preserved by them as a precious possession and, in turn, itself kept them alive by giving them pride in being a chosen people: it was the religion of their primal father to which were attached their hope of reward, of distinction and finally of world-dominion. This last wishful phantasy, long abandoned by the Jewish people, still survives among that people's enemies in a belief in a conspiracy by the 'Elders of Zion'. We reserve for discussion in later pages how the special peculiarities of the monotheist religion borrowed from Egypt affected the Jewish people and how it was bound to leave a permanent imprint on their character through its

[1] ['I believe because it is absurd.' Attributed to Tertullian. This had been discussed by Freud in *The Future of an Illusion* (1927*c*), *Standard Ed.*, **21**, 28–9.]

[2] [See p. 127 ff. below.]

rejection of magic and mysticism, its invitation to advances in intellectuality[1] and its encouragement of sublimations; how the people, enraptured by the possession of the truth, overwhelmed by the consciousness of being chosen, came to have a high opinion of what is intellectual and to lay stress on what is moral; and how their melancholy destinies and their disappointments in reality served only to intensify all these trends. For the moment we will follow their development in another direction.

The re-establishment of the primal father in his historic rights was a great step forward but it could not be the end. The other portions of the prehistoric tragedy insisted on being recognized. It is not easy to discern what set this process in motion. It appears as though a growing sense of guilt had taken hold of the Jewish people, or perhaps of the whole civilized world of the time, as a precursor to the return of the repressed material. Till at last one of these Jewish people found, in justifying a politico-religious agitator, the occasion for detaching a new—the Christian—religion from Judaism. Paul, a Roman Jew from Tarsus, seized upon this sense of guilt and traced it back correctly to its original source. He called this the 'original sin'; it was a crime against God and could only be atoned for by death. With the original sin death came into the world. In fact this crime deserving death had been the murder of the primal father who was later deified. But the murder was not remembered: instead of it there was a phantasy of its atonement, and for that reason this phantasy could be hailed as a message of redemption (*evangelium*). A son of God had allowed himself to be killed without guilt and had thus taken on himself the guilt of all men. It had to be a son, since it had been the murder of a father. It is probable that traditions from oriental and Greek mysteries had had an influence on the phantasy of redemption. What was essential in it seems to have been Paul's own contribution. In the most proper sense he was a man of an innately

[1] ['The Advance in Intellectuality' is the title of Section C of Part II of this essay (p. 111 below). The German word here translated 'intellectuality' is '*Geistigkeit*' and its rendering raises much difficulty. The obvious alternative would be 'spirituality', but in English this arouses some very different associations. The best plan, perhaps, is to examine Freud's own account of the concept in the Section just referred to and to form one's conclusions on that.]

religious disposition: the dark traces of the past lurked in his mind, ready to break through into its more conscious regions.

That the redeemer had sacrificed himself without guilt was evidently a tendentious distortion, which offered difficulties to logical understanding. For how could someone guiltless of the act of murder take on himself the guilt of the murderers by allowing himself to be killed? In the historical reality there was no such contradiction. The 'redeemer' could be none other than the most guilty person, the ringleader of the company of brothers who had overpowered their father. We must in my judgement leave it undecided whether there was such a chief rebel and ringleader. That is possible; but we must also bear in mind that each one of the company of brothers certainly had a wish to commit the deed by himself alone and so to create an exceptional position for himself and to find a substitute for his identification with the father which was having to be given up and which was becoming merged in the community. If there was no such ringleader, then Christ was the heir to a wishful phantasy which remained unfulfilled; if there was one, then he was his successor and his reincarnation. But no matter whether what we have here is a phantasy or the return of a forgotten reality, in any case the origin of the concept of a hero is to be found at this point—the hero who always rebels against his father and kills him in some shape or other.[1] Here too is the true basis for the 'tragic guilt' of the hero of drama, which is otherwise hard to explain. It can scarcely be doubted that the hero and chorus in Greek drama represent the same rebellious hero and company of brothers; and it is not without significance that in the Middle Ages what the theatre started with afresh was the representation of the story of the Passion.

We have already said that the Christian ceremony of Holy Communion, in which the believer incorporates the Saviour's blood and flesh, repeats the content of the old totem meal—no doubt only in its affectionate meaning, expressive of veneration, and not in its aggressive meaning. The ambivalence that dominates the relation to the father was clearly shown, however, in the final outcome of the religious novelty. Ostensibly aimed

[1] Ernest Jones has pointed out that the god Mithras, who kills the bull, might represent this ringleader boasting of his deed. It is well known for how long the worship of Mithras struggled with the young Christianity for the final victory.

at propitiating the father god, it ended in his being dethroned and got rid of. Judaism had been a religion of the father; Christianity became a religion of the son. The old God the Father fell back behind Christ; Christ, the Son, took his place, just as every son had hoped to do in primaeval times. Paul, who carried Judaism on, also destroyed it. No doubt he owed his success in the first instance to the fact that, through the idea of the redeemer, he exorcized humanity's sense of guilt; but he owed it as well to the circumstance that he abandoned the 'chosen' character of his people and its visible mark—circumcision—so that the new religion could be a universal one, embracing all men. Though a part may have been played in Paul's taking this step by his personal desire for revenge for the rejection of his innovation in Jewish circles, yet it also restored a feature of the old Aten religion—it removed a restriction which that religion had acquired when it was handed over to a new vehicle, the Jewish people.

In some respects the new religion meant a cultural regression as compared with the older, Jewish one, as regularly happens when a new mass of people, of a lower level, break their way in or are given admission. The Christian religion did not maintain the high level in things of the mind to which Judaism had soared. It was no longer strictly monotheist, it took over numerous symbolic rituals from surrounding peoples, it re-established the great mother-goddess and found room to introduce many of the divine figures of polytheism only lightly veiled, though in subordinate positions. Above all, it did not, like the Aten religion and the Mosaic one which followed it, exclude the entry of superstitious, magical and mystical elements, which were to prove a severe inhibition upon the intellectual development of the next two thousand years.

The triumph of Christianity was a fresh victory for the priests of Amun over Akhenaten's god after an interval of fifteen hundred years and on a wider stage. And yet in the history of religion—that is, as regards the return of the repressed—Christianity was an advance and from that time on the Jewish religion was to some extent a fossil.

It would be worth while to understand how it was that the monotheist idea made such a deep impression precisely on the Jewish people and that they were able to maintain it so tenaciously. It is possible, I think, to find an answer. Fate had brought the great deed and misdeed of primaeval days, the killing of the father, closer to the Jewish people by causing them to repeat it on the person of Moses, an outstanding father-figure. It was a case of 'acting out' instead of remembering, as happens so often with neurotics during the work of analysis.[1] To the suggestion that they should remember, which was made to them by the doctrine of Moses, they reacted, however, by disavowing their action; they remained halted at the recognition of the great father and thus blocked their access to the point from which Paul was later to start his continuation of the primal history. It is scarcely a matter of indifference or of chance that the violent killing of another great man became the starting-point of Paul's new religious creation as well. This was a man whom a small number of adherents in Judaea regarded as the Son of God and as the Messiah who had been announced, and to whom, too, a part of the childhood story invented for Moses was later carried over [p. 14], but of whom in fact we know scarcely more with certainty than of Moses—whether he was really the great teacher portrayed by the Gospels or whether, rather, it was not the fact and circumstances of his death which were decisive for the importance which his figure acquired. Paul, who became his apostle, had not known him himself.

The killing of Moses by his Jewish people, recognized by Sellin from traces of it in tradition (and also, strange to say, accepted by the young Goethe without any evidence[2]) thus becomes an indispensable part of our construction, an important link between the forgotten event of primaeval times and its later emergence in the form of the monotheist religions.[3] It is plausible to conjecture that remorse for the murder of Moses provided the stimulus for the wishful phantasy of the Messiah, who was to return and lead his people to redemption and the promised world-dominion. If Moses was this first Messiah, Christ became his substitute and successor, and Paul could exclaim to the peoples with some historical justification: 'Look!

[1] [See Freud's technical paper 'Remembering, Repeating and Working-through' (1914*g*), *Standard Ed.*, **12**, 150-4.]

[2] 'Israel in der Wüste' ['Israel in the Wilderness']. In the Weimar Edition, **7**, 170.

[3] On this subject see Frazer's well-known discussions in Part III of *The Golden Bough* (*The Dying God*). [Frazer, 1911.]

the Messiah has really come: he has been murdered before your eyes!' Then, too, there is a piece of historical truth in Christ's resurrection, for he was the resurrected Moses and behind him the returned primal father of the primitive horde, transfigured and, as the son, put in the place of the father.[1]

The poor Jewish people, who with their habitual stubbornness continued to disavow the father's murder, atoned heavily for it in the course of time. They were constantly met with the reproach 'You killed our God!' And this reproach is true, if it is correctly translated. If it is brought into relation with the history of religions, it runs: 'You will not *admit* that you murdered God (the primal picture of God, the primal father, and his later reincarnations).' There should be an addition declaring: 'We did the same thing, to be sure, but we have *admitted* it and since then we have been absolved.' Not all the reproaches with which anti-semitism persecutes the descendants of the Jewish people can appeal to a similar justification. A phenomenon of such intensity and permanence as the people's hatred of the Jews must of course have more than one ground. It is possible to find a whole number of grounds, some of them clearly derived from reality, which call for no interpretation, and others, lying deeper and derived from hidden sources, which might be regarded as the specific reasons. Of the former, the reproach of being aliens is perhaps the weakest, since in many places dominated by anti-semitism to-day the Jews were among the oldest portions of the population or had even been there before the present inhabitants. This applies, for instance, to the city of Cologne, to which the Jews came with the Romans, before it was occupied by the Teutons.[2] Other grounds for hating the Jews are stronger—thus, the circumstances that they live for the most part as minorities among other peoples, for the communal feeling of groups requires, in order to complete it, hostility towards some extraneous minority, and the numerical weakness of this excluded minority encourages its suppression. There are, however, two other char-

[1] [In *G.W.*, **16**,, 196, the words 'the resurrected Moses and behind him' are omitted from this sentence.]

[2] [It will be recalled that in his *Autobiographical Study* (1925*d*), Freud mentions a tradition that his father's family were settled for a long time at Cologne (*Standard Ed.*, **20**, 7–8).]

acteristics of the Jews which are quite unforgivable. First is the fact that in some respects they are different from their 'host' nations. They are not fundamentally different, for they are not Asiatics of a foreign race, as their enemies maintain, but composed for the most part of remnants of the Mediterranean peoples and heirs of the Mediterranean civilization. But they are none the less different, often in an indefinable way different, especially from the Nordic peoples, and the intolerance of groups is often, strangely enough, exhibited more strongly against small differences than against fundamental ones.[1] The other point has a still greater effect: namely, that they defy all oppression, that the most cruel persecutions have not succeeded in exterminating them, and, indeed, that on the contrary they show a capacity for holding their own in commercial life and, where they are admitted, for making valuable contributions to every form of cultural activity.

The deeper motives for hatred of the Jews are rooted in the remotest past ages; they operate from the unconscious of the peoples, and I am prepared to find that at first they will not seem credible. I venture to assert that jealousy of the people which declared itself the first-born, favourite child of God the Father, has not yet been surmounted among other peoples even to-day: it is as though they had thought there was truth in the claim. Further, among the customs by which the Jews made themselves separate, that of circumcision has made a disagreeable, uncanny impression, which is to be explained, no doubt, by its recalling the dreaded castration and along with it a portion of the primaeval past which is gladly forgotten. And finally, as the latest motive in this series, we must not forget that all those peoples who excel to-day in their hatred of Jews became Christians only in late historic times, often driven to it by bloody coercion. It might be said that they are all 'misbaptized'. They have been left, under a thin veneer of Christianity, what their ancestors were, who worshipped a barbarous polytheism. They have not got over a grudge against the new religion which was imposed on them; but they have displaced the grudge on to the source from which Christianity reached them. The fact that the Gospels tell a story which is set among

[1] [Cf. 'the narcissism of minor differences', in Chapter V of *Civilization and its Discontents* (1930*a*), *Standard Ed.*, **21**, 114, where anti-semitism is also discussed.]

Jews, and in fact deals only with Jews, has made this displacement easy for them. Their hatred of Jews is at bottom a hatred of Christians, and we need not be surprised that in the German National-Socialist revolution this intimate relation between the two monotheist religions finds such a clear expression in the hostile treatment of both of them.[1]

E

Difficulties

Perhaps by what I have said I have succeeded in establishing the analogy between neurotic processes and religious events and in thus indicating the unsuspected origin of the latter. In this transference from individual to group psychology two difficulties arise, differing in their nature and importance, to which we must now turn.

The first of these is that we have here dealt with only a single instance from the copious phenomenology of religions and have thrown no light on any others. I must regretfully admit that I am unable to give more than this one example and that my expert knowledge is insufficient to complete the enquiry. From my limited information I may perhaps add that the case of the founding of the Mahommedan religion seems to me like an abbreviated repetition of the Jewish one, of which it emerged as an imitation. It appears, indeed, that the Prophet intended originally to accept Judaism completely for himself and his people. The recapture of the single great primal father brought the Arabs an extraordinary exaltation of their self-confidence, which led to great worldly successes but exhausted itself in them. Allah showed himself far more grateful to his chosen people than Yahweh did to his. But the internal development

[1] [Freud seems to have first mentioned the unconscious root of anti-semitism in the castration complex and circumcision in a footnote to his 'Little Hans' case history (1909*b*), *Standard Ed.*, **10,** 36 *n.* He repeated the point in a footnote added in 1919 to his study of Leonardo (1910*c*), ibid., **11,** 95–6 *n.* A reference to anti-semitism in *Civilization and its Discontents* has been mentioned above (p. 91) in an Editor's footnote. The present discussion, is, however, much more elaborate than any of these. The subject was once again the topic of Freud's short contribution to a Paris periodical (1938*a*), *Standard Ed.*, **23,** 291.]

of the new religion soon came to a stop, perhaps because it lacked the depth which had been caused in the Jewish case by the murder of the founder of their religion. The apparently rationalistic religions of the East are in their core ancestor-worship and so come to a halt, too, at an early stage of the reconstruction of the past. If it is true that in primitive peoples of to-day the recognition of a supreme being is the only content of their religion, we can only regard this as an atrophy of religious development and bring it into relation with the countless cases of rudimentary neuroses which are to be observed in the other field. Why it is that in the one case just as in the other things have gone no further, our knowledge is in both cases insufficient to tell us. We can only attribute the responsibility to the individual endowment of these peoples, the direction taken by their activity and their general social condition. Moreover, it is a good rule in the work of analysis to be content to explain what is actually before one and not to seek to explain what has *not* happened.

The second difficulty about this transference to group psychology is far more important, because it poses a fresh problem of a fundamental nature. It raises the question in what form the operative tradition in the life of peoples is present—a question which does not occur with individuals, since there it is solved by the existence in the unconscious of memory-traces of the past. Let us return to our historical example. We have attributed the compromise at Kadesh to the survival of a powerful tradition among those who had returned from Egypt. This case involves no problem. According to our theory, a tradition of this kind was based on conscious memories of oral communications which people then living had received from their ancestors only two or three generations back who had themselves been participants and eye-witnesses of the events in question. But can we believe the same thing of the later centuries—that the tradition still had its basis in a knowledge normally handed on from grandfather to grandchild? It is no longer possible to say, as it was in the earlier case, who the people were who preserved this knowledge and handed it on by word of mouth. According to Sellin the tradition of the murder of Moses was always in the possession of priestly circles till eventually it found expression in writing which alone enabled Sellin to discover it. But it can only have been known to a few people; it was not public property.

And is that enough to explain its effect? Is it possible to attribute to knowledge held like this by a few people the power to produce such a lasting emotion in the masses when it came to their notice? It seems, rather, as though there must have been something present in the ignorant masses, too, which was in some way akin to the knowledge of the few and went half way to meet it when it was uttered.

A decision is made still more difficult when we turn to the analogous case in primaeval times. It is quite certain that in the course of thousands of years the fact was forgotten that there had been a primal father with the characteristics we know and what his fate had been; nor can we suppose that there was any oral tradition of it, as we can in the case of Moses. In what sense, then, does a tradition come in question at all? In what form can it have been present?

In order to make it easier for readers who do not desire or are not prepared to plunge into a complicated psychological state of affairs, I will anticipate the outcome of the investigation that is to follow. In my opinion there is an almost complete conformity in this respect between the individual and the group: in the group too an impression of the past is retained in unconscious memory-traces.

In the case of the individual we believe we can see clearly. The memory-trace of his early experience has been preserved in him, but in a special psychological condition. The individual may be said to have known it always, just as one knows about the repressed. Here we have formed ideas, which can be confirmed without difficulty through analysis, of how something can be forgotten and how it can then reappear after a while. What is forgotten is not extinguished but only 'repressed'; its memory-traces are present in all their freshness, but isolated by 'anticathexes'. They cannot enter into communication with other intellectual processes; they are unconscious—inaccessible to consciousness. It may also be that certain portions of the repressed, having evaded the process [of repression], remain accessible to memory and occasionally emerge into consciousness; but even so they are isolated, like foreign bodies out of connection with the rest. It may be so, but it need not be so; repression may also be complete, and it is with that alternative that we shall deal in what follows.

The repressed retains its upward urge, its effort to force its way to consciousness. It achieves its aim under three conditions: (1) if the strength of the anticathexis is diminished by pathological processes which overtake the other part [of the mind], what we call the ego, or by a different distribution of the cathectic energies in that ego, as happens regularly in the state of sleep; (2) if the instinctual elements attaching to the repressed receive a special reinforcement (of which the best example is the processes during puberty); and (3) if at any time in recent experience impressions or experiences occur which resemble the repressed so closely that they are able to awaken it. In the last case the recent experience is reinforced by the latent energy of the repressed, and the repressed comes into operation behind the recent experience and with its help. In none of these three alternatives does what has hitherto been repressed enter consciousness smoothly and unaltered; it must always put up with distortions which testify to the influence of the resistance (not entirely overcome) arising from the anticathexis, or to the modifying influence of the recent experience or to both.

The difference between whether a psychical process is conscious or unconscious has served us as a criterion and a means of finding our bearings. The repressed is unconscious. Now it would simplify things agreeably if this sentence admitted of reversal—if, that is, the difference between the qualities of conscious (*Cs.*) and unconscious (*Ucs.*) coincided with the distinction between 'belonging to the ego' and 'repressed'.[1] The fact of there being isolated and unconscious things like this in our mental life would be sufficiently novel and important. But in reality the position is more complicated. It is true that everything repressed is unconscious, but it is not true that

[1] [It may be remarked that these abbreviations make their final appearance here after a long interval. Apart from a couple of occurrences in Lecture XXXI of the *New Introductory Lectures* (1933*a*), *Standard Ed.*, **22**, 71–2, they had fallen entirely out of use since the structural account of the mind was established some fifteen years earlier in *The Ego and the Id* (1923*b*), where a full discussion of them is given in the Editor's Introduction, *Standard Ed.*, **19**, 4 ff. It is a curious fact that in the present work they are used, quite contrary to Freud's normal practice, in a 'descriptive' sense. These abbreviations are in fact also used in the manuscript of the *Outline of Psycho-Analysis* (1940*a*). Abbrevitions of all kinds are however especially frequent in that manuscript and the work, of course, was not seen by Freud in print.]

everything belonging to the ego is conscious. We notice that consciousness is a transient quality which attaches to a psychical process only in passing. For our purposes therefore we must replace 'conscious' by 'capable of being conscious' and we call this quality 'preconscious' (*Pcs.*). We then say, more correctly, that the ego is mainly preconscious (virtually conscious) but that portions of the ego are unconscious.

The establishment of this latter fact shows us that the qualities on which we have hitherto relied are insufficient to give us our bearings in the obscurity of mental life. We must introduce another distinction which is no longer qualitative but *topographical* and—what gives it special value—at the same time *genetic*. We now distinguish in our mental life (which we regard as an apparatus compounded of several agencies, districts or provinces) one region which we call the *ego* proper and another which we name the *id*. The id is the older of the two; the ego has developed out of it, like a cortical layer, through the influence of the external world. It is in the id that all our primary instincts are at work, all the processes in the id take place unconsciously. The ego, as we have already said, coincides with the region of the preconscious; it includes portions which normally remain unconscious. The course of events in the id, and their mutual interaction, are governed by quite other laws than those prevailing in the ego. It is in fact the discovery of these differences that has led to our new view and justifies it.

The *repressed* is to be counted as belonging to the id and is subject to the same mechanisms; it is distinguished from it only in respect to its genesis. The differentiation is accomplished in the earliest period of life, while the ego is developing out of the id. At that time a portion of the contents of the id is taken into the ego and raised to the preconscious state; another portion is not affected by this translation and remains behind in the id as the unconscious proper. In the further course of the formation of the ego, however, certain psychical impressions and processes in the ego are excluded [i.e. expelled] from it by a defensive process; the characteristic of being preconscious is withdrawn from them, so that they are once more reduced to being component portions of the id. Here then is the 'repressed' in the id. So far as intercourse between the two mental provinces is concerned, we therefore assume that, on the one hand, unconscious processes in the id are raised to the level of the preconscious and incorporated into the ego, and that, on the other hand, preconscious material in the ego can follow the opposite path and be put back into the id. The fact that later on a special region —that of the 'super-ego'—is separated off in the ego lies outside our present interest.[1]

All of this may appear to be far from simple.[2] But when one has grown reconciled to this unusual spatial view of the mental apparatus, it can present no particular difficulties to the imagination. I will add the further comment that the psychical topography that I have developed here has nothing to do with the anatomy of the brain, and actually only touches it at one point.[3] What is unsatisfactory in this picture—and I am aware of it as clearly as anyone—is due to our complete ignorance of the *dynamic* nature of the mental processes. We tell ourselves that what distinguishes a conscious idea from a preconscious one, and the latter from an unconscious one, can only be a modification, or perhaps a different distribution, of psychical energy. We talk of cathexes and hypercathexes, but beyond this we are without any knowledge on the subject or even any starting-point for a serviceable working hypothesis. Of the phenomenon of consciousness we can at least say that it was originally attached to perception. All sensations which originate from the perception of painful, tactile, auditory or visual stimuli are what are most readily conscious. Thought-processes, and whatever may be analogous to them in the id, are in themselves unconscious and obtain access to consciousness by becoming linked to the mnemic residues of visual and auditory perceptions along the path of the function of speech.[4] In animals, which lack speech, these conditions must be of a simpler kind.

The impressions of early traumas, from which we started out, are either not translated into the preconscious or are quickly

[1] [Some discussion of the super-ego will however be found below (p. 116 f.).]

[2] [A fuller account is given in Lecture XXXI of the *New Introductory Lectures* (1933*a*).]

[3] [This single point, as Freud explains in parallel accounts in *Beyond the Pleasure Principle* (1920*g*), *Standard Ed.*, **18**, 24 and *The Ego and the Id* (1923*b*), ibid., **19**, 19, lies in the perceptual system, which is regarded as cortical both in anatomy and in Freud's metapsychology.]

[4] [For a long technical discussion of this see Part VII of the metapsychological paper on 'The Unconscious' (1915*e*), *Standard Ed.*, **14**, 201 ff.]

put back by repression into the id-condition. Their mnemic residues are in that case unconscious and operate from the id. We believe we can easily follow their further vicissitudes so long as it is a question of what has been experienced by the subject himself. But a fresh complication arises when we become aware of the probability that what may be operative in an individual's psychical life may include not only what he has experienced himself but also things that were innately present in him at his birth, elements with a phylogenetic origin—an *archaic heritage*. The questions then arise of what this consists in, what it contains and what is the evidence for it.

The immediate and most certain answer is that it consists in certain [innate] dispositions such as are characteristic of all living organisms: in the capacity and tendency, that is, to enter particular lines of development and to react in a particular manner to certain excitations, impressions and stimuli. Since experience shows that there are distinctions in this respect between individuals of the human species, the archaic heritage must include these distinctions; they represent what we recognize as the *constitutional* factor in the individual. Now, since all human beings, at all events in their early days, have approximately the same experiences, they react to them, too, in a similar manner; a doubt was therefore able to arise whether we should not include these reactions, along with their individual distinctions, in the archaic heritage. This doubt should be put on one side: our knowledge of the archaic heritage is not enlarged by the fact of this similarity.

Nevertheless, analytic research has brought us a few results which give us cause for thought. There is, in the first place, the universality of symbolism in language. The symbolic representation of one object by another—the same thing applies to actions—is familiar to all our children and comes to them, as it were, as a matter of course. We cannot show in regard to them how they have learnt it and must admit that in many cases learning it is impossible. It is a question of an original knowledge which adults afterwards forget. It is true that an adult makes use of the same symbols in his dreams, but he does not understand them unless an analyst interprets them to him, and even then he is reluctant to believe the translation. If he makes use of one of the very common figures of speech in which this symbolism is recorded, he is obliged to admit that its true sense has completely escaped him. Moreover, symbolism disregards differences of language; investigations would probably show that it is ubiquitous—the same for all peoples. Here, then, we seem to have an assured instance of an archaic heritage dating from the period at which language developed. But another explanation might still be attempted. It might be said that we are dealing with thought-connections between ideas—connections which had been established during the historical development of speech and which have to be repeated now every time the development of speech has to be gone through in an individual. It would thus be a case of the inheritance of an intellectual disposition similar to the ordinary inheritance of an instinctual disposition—and once again it would be no contribution to our problem.

The work of analysis has, however, brought something else to light which exceeds in its importance what we have so far considered. When we study the reactions to early traumas, we are quite often surprised to find that they are not strictly limited to what the subject himself has really experienced but diverge from it in a way which fits in much better with the model of a phylogenetic event and, in general, can only be explained by such an influence. The behaviour of neurotic children towards their parents in the Oedipus and castration complex abounds in such reactions, which seem unjustified in the individual case and only become intelligible phylogenetically—by their connection with the experience of earlier generations. It would be well worth while to place this material, which I am able to appeal to here, before the public in a collected form. Its evidential value seems to me strong enough for me to venture on a further step and to posit the assertion that the archaic heritage of human beings comprises not only dispositions but also subject-matter—memory-traces of the experience of earlier generations. In this way the compass as well as the importance of the archaic heritage would be significantly extended.

On further reflection I must admit that I have behaved for a long time as though the inheritance of memory-traces of the experience of our ancestors, independently of direct communication and of the influence of education by the setting of an example, were established beyond question. When I spoke of the survival of a tradition among a people or of the formation of a people's character, I had mostly in mind an inherited tradition of this kind and not one transmitted by communication. Or at least I made no distinction between the two and was not clearly aware of my audacity in neglecting to do so. My position, no doubt, is made more difficult by the present attitude of biological science, which refuses to hear of the inheritance of acquired characters by succeeding generations. I must, however, in all modesty confess that nevertheless I cannot do without this factor in biological evolution. The same thing is not in question, indeed, in the two cases: in the one it is a matter of acquired characters which are hard to grasp, in the other of memory-traces of external events—something tangible, as it were. But it may well be that at bottom we cannot imagine one without the other.

If we assume the survival of these memory-traces in the archaic heritage, we have bridged the gulf between individual and group psychology: we can deal with peoples as we do with an individual neurotic. Granted that at the time we have no stronger evidence for the presence of memory-traces in the archaic heritage than the residual phenomena of the work of analysis which call for a phylogenetic derivation, yet this evidence seems to us strong enough to postulate that such is the fact. If it is not so, we shall not advance a step further along the path we entered on, either in analysis or in group psychology. The audacity cannot be avoided.

And by this assumption we are effecting something else. We are diminishing the gulf which earlier periods of human arrogance had torn too wide apart between mankind and the animals. If any explanation is to be found of what are called the instincts[1] of animals, which allow them to behave from the first in a new situation in life as though it were an old and familiar one—if any explanation at all is to be found of this instinctive life of animals, it can only be that they bring the experiences of their species with them into their own new existence—that is, that they have preserved memories of what was experienced by their ancestors. The position in the human animal would not at bottom be different. His own archaic heritage corresponds to the instincts of animals even though it is different in its compass and contents.

[1] [Here and in the remainder of this paragraph the German word is '*Instinkt*' and not '*Trieb*'. Similarly on p. 133 below.]

After this discussion I have no hesitation in declaring that men have always known (in this special way) that they once possessed a primal father and killed him.

Two further questions must now be answered. First, under what conditions does a memory of this kind enter the archaic heritage? And, secondly, in what circumstances can it become active—that is, can it advance to consciousness from its unconscious state in the id, even though in an altered and distorted shape? The answer to the first question is easy to formulate: the memory enters the archaic heritage if the event was important enough, or repeated often enough, or both. In the case of parricide both conditions are fulfilled. On the second question there is this to be said. A whole number of influences may be concerned, not all of which are necessarily known. A spontaneous development is also conceivable, on the analogy of what happens in some neuroses. What is certainly of decisive importance, however, is the awakening of the forgotten memory-trace by a recent real repetition of the event. The murder of Moses was a repetition of this kind and, later, the supposed judicial murder of Christ: so that these events come into the foreground as causes. It seems as though the genesis of monotheism could not do without these occurrences. We are reminded of the poet's words:

> Was unsterblich im Gesang soll leben,
> Muss im Leben untergehn.[1]

And lastly a remark which brings up a psychological argument. A tradition that was based only on communication could not lead to the compulsive character that attaches to religious phenomena. It would be listened to, judged, and perhaps dismissed, like any other piece of information from outside; it would never attain the privilege of being liberated from the constraint of logical thought. It must have undergone the fate of being repressed, the condition of lingering in the unconscious, before it is able to display such powerful effects on its return, to bring the masses under its spell, as we have seen with astonishment and hitherto without comprehension in the case of religious tradition. And this consideration weighs heavily in

[1] [Literally: 'What is to live immortal in song must perish in life.'] Schiller, 'Die Götter Griechenlands'.

favour of our believing that things really happened in the way we have tried to picture them or at least in some similar way.[1]

[1] [The discussion of the 'archaic heritage' in this section is by far the longest in Freud's writings. The question of the relative parts played in mental life by heredity and experience was, of course, a repeated topic for discussion from the earliest times. But this particular point of the possibility of the inheritance of actual ancestral experiences had appeared relatively late in Freud's writings. The problem of the transmission of ancestral experiences was necessarily raised in *Totem and Taboo* (1912–1913). 'What are the ways and means', Freud asks there, 'employed by one generation in order to hand on its mental states to the next one?' (*Standard Ed.*, **13**, 158.) His reply in this passage is non-committal, though he seems to suggest that the process can be accounted for by conscious and unconscious communication from one generation to another. But it is not difficult to see that even then he had other ideas at the back of his mind. Indeed, the possibility of the inheritance of an 'archaic constitution as an atavistic vestige' is explicitly mentioned there in connection with ambivalence (ibid., **13**, 66), and, in this same connection, the term '*archaisches Erbteil*' (translated 'archaic inheritance') appears in 'Instincts and their Vicissitudes' (1915*c*), ibid., **14**, 131. It seems probable that these ideas were precipitated (like so much else) in connection with the 'Wolf Man' analysis and particularly with the topic of 'primal phantasies'. This analysis was actually in progress while Freud was writing *Totem and Taboo* and his first draft of the case history was written in 1914. The possibility of a 'phylogenetic heritage' had, however, also arisen in connection with symbolism. This question was discussed somewhat allusively in Lecture X of the *Introductory Lectures, Standard Ed.*, **15**, 165–6, and more explicitly in a sentence near the beginning of Lecture XIII, ibid., 199. The first definite reference to the inheritance of primal phantasies seems to have been in Lecture XXIII of the *Introductory Lectures* (1917), *Standard Ed.*, **16**, 371, but it was further developed in one of the passages added after this to the 'Wolf Man' case history (*Standard Ed.*, **17**, 97). The actual term '*archaische Erbschaft*' seems to appear for the first time in 1919—in a paragraph added in that year to Chapter VII (B) of *The Interpretation of Dreams, Standard Ed.*, **5**, 548–9, in 'A Child is Being Beaten', ibid., **17**, 203 and in Freud's preface to Reik's book on religious origins, ibid., **17**, 262. Thereafter the concept and the term appear frequently, though only in Chapter III of *The Ego and the Id* is the subject discussed at any length (ibid., **19**, 36–8). (A late reference to the question will be found in Section VI of 'Analysis Terminable and Interminable' (1937*c*), ibid., **23**, 240.) The whole question of Freud's views on the inheritance of acquired characters is discussed by Ernest Jones in Chapter 10 of Vol. III of his life of Freud (1957).]

PART II

Summary and Recapitulation

The part of this study which follows cannot be given to the public without extensive explanations and apologies. For it is nothing other than a faithful (and often word-for-word) repetition of the first part [of the third Essay], abbreviated in some of its critical enquiries and augmented by additions relating to the problem of how the special character of the Jewish people arose. I am aware that a method of exposition such as this is no less inexpedient than it is inartistic. I myself deplore it unreservedly. Why have I not avoided it? The answer to that is not hard for me to find, but it is not easy to confess. I found myself unable to wipe out the traces of the history of the work's origin, which was in any case unusual.

Actually it has been written twice: for the first time a few years ago in Vienna, where I did not think it would be possible to publish it. I determined to give it up; but it tormented me like an unlaid ghost, and I found a way out by making two pieces of it independent and publishing them in our periodical *Imago*: the psycho-analytic starting-point of the whole thing 'Moses an Egyptian' [Essay I], and the historical construction erected on this 'If Moses was an Egyptian . . .' [Essay II]. The remainder, which included what was really open to objection and dangerous—the application [of these findings] to the genesis of monotheism and the view of religion in general—I held back, as I thought, for ever. Then, in March 1938, came the unexpected German invasion, which forced me to leave my home but also freed me from my anxiety lest my publication might conjure up a prohibition of psycho-analysis in a place where it was still tolerated. I had scarcely arrived in England before I found the temptation irresistible to make the knowledge I had held back accessible to the world, and I began to revise the third part of my study to fit it on to the two parts that had already been published. This naturally involved a partial rearrangement of the material. I did not succeed, however, in including the whole of this material in my second version; on the other hand I could not make up my mind to give up the earlier versions entirely. And so it has come about that I have adopted the expedient of attaching a whole piece of the first presentation to the second unchanged—which has brought with it the disadvantage of involving extensive repetition.

I might, however, console myself with the reflection that the things I am treating are in any case so new and so important, apart from how far my account of them is correct, that it can be no misfortune if the public is obliged to read the same thing about them twice over. There are things which should be said more than once and which cannot be said often enough. But the reader must decide of his own free will whether to linger over the subject or to come back to it. He must not be surreptitiously led into having the same thing put before him twice in one book. It is a piece of clumsiness for which the author must take the blame. Unluckily an author's creative power does not always obey his will: the work proceeds as it can, and often presents itself to the author as something independent or even alien.[1]

[1] [Freud had said something similar at rather greater length near the beginning of Lecture XXIV of the *Introductory Lectures*, *Standard Ed.*, **16**, 379.]

A

The People of Israel

If we are clear in our mind that a procedure like ours of accepting what seems to us serviceable in the material presented to us and of rejecting what does not suit us and of putting the different pieces together in accordance with psychological probability—if we are clear that a technique of this kind can give no certainty that we shall arrive at the truth, then it may justly be asked why we are undertaking this work at all. The answer is an appeal to the work's outcome. If we greatly tone down the strictness of the requirements made upon a historico-psychological investigation, it will perhaps be possible to throw light on problems which have always seemed to deserve attention and which recent events have forced upon our observation anew. As we know, of all the peoples who lived round the basin of the Mediterranean in antiquity, the Jewish people is almost the only one which still exists in name and also in substance. It has met misfortunes and ill-treatment with an unexampled capacity for resistance; it has developed special character-traits and incidentally has earned the hearty dislike of every other people. We should be glad to understand more of the source of this viability of the Jews and of how their characteristics are connected with their history.

We may start from a character-trait of the Jews which dominates their relation to others. There is no doubt that they have a particularly high opinion of themselves, that they regard themselves as more distinguished, of higher standing, as superior to other peoples—from whom they are also distinguished by many of their customs.[1] At the same time they are inspired by a peculiar confidence in life, such as is derived from the secret ownership of some precious possession, a kind of optimism: pious people would call it trust in God.

We know the reason for this behaviour and what their secret

[1] The aspersion, so common in antiquity, that the Jews were 'lepers' (cf. Manetho [*History of Egypt*, English translation, 1940, 119 ff.]) no doubt has the sense of a projection: 'they keep as much apart from us as though we were lepers.'

treasure is. They really regard themselves as God's chosen people, they believe that they stand especially close to him; and this makes them proud and confident. Trustworthy reports tell us that they behaved in Hellenistic times just as they do to-day, so that the complete Jew was already there; and the Greeks, among whom and alongside of whom they lived, reacted to the Jewish characteristics in the same way as their 'hosts' do to-day. It might be thought that they reacted as though they too believed in the superiority which the people of Israel claimed for themselves. If one is the declared favourite of the dreaded father, one need not be surprised at the jealousy of one's brothers and sisters, and the Jewish legend of Joseph and his brethren shows very well where this jealousy can lead. The course of world-history seemed to justify the presumption of the Jews, since, when later on it pleased God to send mankind a Messiah and redeemer, he once again chose him from the Jewish people. The other peoples might have had occasion then to say to themselves: 'Indeed, they were right, they *are* God's chosen people.' But instead of this, what happened was that redemption by Jesus Christ only intensified their hatred of the Jews, while the Jews themselves gained no advantage from this second act of favouritism, since they did not recognize the redeemer.

On the basis of our earlier discussions, we may now assert that it was the man Moses who imprinted this trait—significant for all time—upon the Jewish people. He raised their self-esteem by assuring them that they were God's chosen people, he enjoined them to holiness [p. 120] and pledged them to be apart from others. Not that other peoples were lacking in self-esteem. Just as to-day, so in those days each nation thought itself better than any other. But the self-esteem of the Jews was given a religious anchorage by Moses: it became a part of their religious faith. Owing to their especially intimate relation to their God they acquired a share in his grandeur. And since we know that behind the God who had chosen the Jews and freed them from Egypt stands the figure of Moses, who had done precisely that, ostensibly at God's command, we venture to declare that it was this one man Moses who created the Jews. It is to him that this people owes its tenacity of life but also much of the hostility it has experienced and still experiences.

B

The Great Man

How is it possible for a single man to evolve such extraordinary effectiveness that he can form a people out of random individuals and families, can stamp them with their definitive character and determine their fate for thousands of years? Is not a hypothesis such as this a relapse into the mode of thought which led to myths of a creator and to the worship of heroes, into times in which the writing of history was nothing more than a report of the deeds and destinies of single individuals, of rulers or conquerors? The modern tendency is rather towards tracing back the events of human history to more concealed, general and impersonal factors, to the compelling influence of economic conditions, to alterations in food habits, to advances in the use of materials and tools, to migrations brought about by increases in population and climatic changes. Individuals have no other part to play in this than as exponents or representatives of group trends, which are bound to find expression and do so in these particular individuals largely by chance.

These are perfectly justifiable lines of approach, but they give us occasion for drawing attention to an important discrepancy between the attitude taken up by our organ of thought and the arrangement of things in the world, which are supposed to be grasped by means of our thought. It is enough for our need to discover causes (which, to be sure, is imperative) if each event has *one* demonstrable cause.[1] But in the reality lying outside us that is scarcely the case; on the contrary, each event seems to be overdetermined and proves to be the effect of several convergent causes. Frightened by the immense complication of events, our investigations take the side of one correlation as against another and set up contradictions which do not exist but have only arisen owing to a rupture of more comprehensive

[1] [Freud had made this point before in the third of his *Five Lectures* (1910*a*), *Standard Ed.*, **11**, 38.—The fact of multiple causation was constantly insisted on by him from early times. See, for instance, Chapter IV, Section 1, of *Studies on Hysteria* (1895*d*), *Standard Ed.*, **2**, 263.]

relations.[1] Accordingly, if the investigation of a particular case demonstrates to us the transcendent influence of a single personality, our conscience need not reproach us with having by this hypothesis flown in the face of the doctrine of the importance of the general and impersonal factors. There is room in principle for both. In the case of the genesis of monotheism, however, we can point to no external factor other than the one we have already mentioned—that this development was linked with the establishment of closer relations between different nations and with the building up of a great empire.

Thus we reserve a place for 'great men' in the chain, or rather the network, of causes. But it may not, perhaps, be quite useless to enquire under what conditions we confer this title of honour. We shall be surprised to find that it is never quite easy to answer this question. A first formulation—'we do so if a man possesses to a specially high degree qualities that we value greatly'—clearly misses the mark in every respect. Beauty, for instance, and muscular strength, however enviable they may be, constitute no claim to 'greatness'. It would seem, then, that the qualities have to be mental ones—psychical and intellectual distinctions. As regards these, we are held up by the consideration that nevertheless we should not unhesitatingly describe someone as a great man simply because he was extraordinarily efficient in some particular sphere. We should certainly not do so in the case of a chess master or of a virtuoso on a musical instrument; but not very easily, either, in the case of a distinguished artist or scientist. In such cases we should naturally speak of him as a great poet, painter, mathematician or physicist, or as a pioneer in the field of this or that activity; but we refrain from pronouncing him a great man. If we unhesitatingly declare that, for instance, Goethe and Leonardo da Vinci and Beethoven were great men, we must be led to it by something other than admiration for their splendid creations. If precisely such examples as these did not stand in the way, the idea would probably occur to us that the name of a 'great man'

[1] I protest, however, against being misunderstood to say that the world is so complicated that any assertion one may make is bound to hit upon a piece of truth somewhere. No. Our thought has upheld its liberty to discover dependent relations and connections to which there is nothing corresponding in reality; and it clearly sets a very high value on this gift, since it makes such copious use of it both inside and outside of science.

is preferably reserved for men of action—conquerors, generals, rulers—and is in recognition of the greatness of their achievement, the force of the effects to which they gave rise. But this too is unsatisfactory and is entirely contradicted by our condemnation of so many worthless figures whose effects upon their contemporary world and upon posterity can nevertheless not be disputed. Nor shall we be able to choose success as a sign of greatness, when we reflect on the majority of great men who instead of achieving success have perished in misfortune.

For the moment, then, we are inclined to decide that it is not worth while to look for a connotation of the concept of a 'great man' that is unambiguously determined. It seems to be only a loosely used and somewhat arbitrarily conferred recognition of an over-large development of certain human qualities, with some approximation to the original literal sense of 'greatness'. We must recollect, too, that we are not so much interested in the essence of great men as in the question of the means by which they affect their fellow-men. We will, however, keep this enquiry as short as possible, since it threatens to lead us far away from our goal.

Let us, therefore, take it for granted that a great man influences his fellow-men in two ways: by his personality and by the idea which he puts forward. That idea may stress some ancient wishful image of the masses, or it may point out a new wishful aim to them, or it may cast its spell over them in some other way. Occasionally—and this is undoubtedly the more primary case—the personality works by itself and the idea plays a quite trivial part. Not for a moment are we in the dark as to why a great man ever becomes important. We know that in the mass of mankind there is a powerful need for an authority who can be admired, before whom one bows down, by whom one is ruled and perhaps even ill-treated. We have learnt from the psychology of individual men what the origin is of this need of the masses. It is a longing for the father felt by everyone from his childhood onwards, for the same father whom the hero of legend boasts he has overcome. And now it may begin to dawn on us that all the characteristics with which we equipped the great man are paternal characteristics, and that the essence of great men for which we vainly searched lies in this conformity. The decisiveness of thought, the strength of will, the energy of action are part of the picture of a father—but above all the autonomy and independence of the great man, his divine unconcern which may grow into ruthlessness. One must admire him, one may trust him, but one cannot avoid being afraid of him too. We should have been led to realize this from the word itself: who but the father can have been the 'great man' in childhood?[1]

There is no doubt that it was a mighty prototype of a father which, in the person of Moses, stooped to the poor Jewish bondsmen to assure them that they were his dear children. And no less overwhelming must have been the effect upon them of the idea of an only, eternal, almighty God, to whom they were not too mean for him to make a covenant with them and who promised to care for them if they remained loyal to his worship. It was probably not easy for them to distinguish the image of the man Moses from that of his God; and their feeling was right in this, for Moses may have introduced traits of his own personality into the character of his God—such as his wrathful temper and his relentlessness. And if, this being so, they killed their great man one day, they were only repeating a misdeed which in ancient times had been committed, as prescribed by law, against the Divine King and which, as we know, went back to a still more ancient prototype.[2]

If on the one hand we thus see the figure of the great man grown to divine proportions, yet on the other hand we must recall that the father too was once a child. The great religious idea for which the man Moses stood was, on our view, not his own property: he had taken it over from King Akhenaten. And he, whose greatness as the founder of a religion is unequivocally established, may perhaps have been following hints which had reached him—from near or distant parts of Asia—through the medium of his mother[3] or by other paths.

We cannot follow the chain of events further, but if we have rightly recognized these first steps, the monotheist idea returned like a boomerang to the land of its origin. Thus it seems unfruitful to try to fix the credit due to an individual in connection with a new idea. It is clear that many have shared in its

[1] [In German '*der grosse Mann*' means not only 'the great man' but 'the tall man' or 'the big man'.]

[2] Cf. Frazer, loc. cit. [See p. 89, footnote 3.]

[3] [The theory held at one time, that Akhenaten's mother, Queen Tiye, was of foreign origin, has been abandoned in view of the discovery of her parents' tomb at Thebes.]

development and made contributions to it. And, again, it would obviously be unjust to break off the chain of causes at Moses and to neglect what was effected by those who succeeded him and carried on his ideas, the Jewish Prophets. The seed of monotheism failed to ripen in Egypt. The same thing might have happened in Israel after the people had thrown off the burdensome and exacting religion. But there constantly arose from the Jewish people men who revived the fading tradition, who renewed the admonitions and demands made by Moses, and who did not rest till what was lost had been established once again. In the course of constant efforts over centuries, and finally owing to two great reforms, one before and one after the Babylonian exile, the transformation was accomplished of the popular god Yahweh into the God whose worship had been forced upon the Jews by Moses. And evidence of the presence of a peculiar psychical aptitude in the masses who had become the Jewish people is revealed by the fact that they were able to produce so many individuals prepared to take on the burdens of the religion of Moses in return for the reward of being the chosen people and perhaps for some other prizes of a similar degree.

C

The Advance in Intellectuality[1]

In order to bring about lasting psychical results in a people, it is clearly not enough to *assure* them that they have been chosen by the deity. The fact must also be *proved* to them in some way if they are to believe it and to draw consequences from the belief. In the religion of Moses the Exodus from Egypt served as the proof; God, or Moses in his name, was never tired of appealing to this evidence of favour. The feast of the Passover was introduced in order to maintain the memory of that event, or, rather, an old-established feast was injected with the contents of that memory. Nevertheless, it was only a memory: the

[1] [This Section, as has been mentioned in the Editor's Note, p. 3, appeared first separately in *Int. Z. Psychoan. Imago*, **24** (1939), 6–9. Two variants from the final version are noted below. For a discussion of the English rendering of the title see the footnote on p. 86 above.]

Exodus belonged to a hazy past. In the present, signs of God's favour were decidedly scanty; the people's history pointed rather to his *dis*favour. Primitive peoples used to depose their gods or even to castigate them, if they failed to do their duty in securing them victory, happiness and comfort. In all periods kings have been treated in no way differently from gods; an ancient identity is thus revealed: an origin from a common root. Thus, modern peoples, too, are in the habit of expelling their kings if the glory of their reign is spoilt by defeats and the corresponding losses in territory and money. Why the people of Israel, however, clung more and more submissively to their God the worse they were treated by him—that is a problem which for the moment we must leave on one side.

It may encourage us to enquire whether the religion of Moses brought the people nothing else besides an enhancement of their self-esteem owing to their consciousness of having been chosen. And indeed another factor can easily be found. That religion also brought the Jews a far grander conception of God, or, as we might put it more modestly, the conception of a grander God. Anyone who believed in this God had some kind of share in his greatness, might feel exalted himself. For an unbeliever this is not entirely self-evident; but we may perhaps make it easier to understand if we point to the sense of superiority felt by a Briton in a foreign country which has been made insecure owing to an insurrection—a feeling that is completely absent in a citizen of any small continental state. For the Briton counts on the fact that his Government[1] will send along a warship if a hair of his head is hurt, and that the rebels understand that very well—whereas the small state possesses no warship at all. Thus, pride in the greatness of the British Empire[2] has a root as well in the consciousness of the greater security—the protection—enjoyed by the individual Briton. This may resemble the conception of a grand God. And, since one can scarcely claim to assist God in the administration of the world, the pride in God's greatness fuses with the pride in being chosen by him.

Among the precepts of the Moses religion there is one that is of greater importance than appears to begin with. This is the prohibition against making an image of God—the compulsion

[1] [In English in the original.]
[2] [Also in English.]

to worship a God whom one cannot see.[1] In this, I suspect, Moses was outdoing the strictness of the Aten religion. Perhaps he merely wanted to be consistent: his God would in that case have neither a name nor a countenance. Perhaps it was a fresh measure against magical abuses.[2] But if this prohibition were accepted, it must have a profound effect. For it meant that a sensory perception was given second place to what may be called an abstract idea—a triumph of intellectuality over sensuality or, strictly speaking, an instinctual renunciation, with all its necessary psychological consequences.

This may not seem obvious at first sight, and before it can carry conviction we must recall other processes of the same character in the development of human civilization. The earliest of these and perhaps the most important is merged in the obscurity of primaeval ages. Its astonishing effects compel us to assert its occurrence. In our children, in adults who are neurotic, as well as in primitive peoples, we meet with the mental phenomenon which we describe as a belief in the 'omnipotence of thoughts'. In our judgement this lies in an over-estimation of the influence which our mental (in this case, intellectual) acts can exercise in altering the external world. At bottom, all magic, the precursor of our technology, rests on this premiss. All the magic of words, too, has its place here, and the conviction of the power which is bound up with the knowledge and pronouncing of a name. The 'omnipotence of thoughts' was, we suppose, an expression of the pride of mankind in the development of speech, which resulted in such an extraordinary advancement of intellectual activities. The new realm of intellectuality was opened up, in which ideas, memories and inferences became decisive in contrast to the lower psychical activity which had direct perceptions by the sense-organs as its content. This was unquestionably one of the most important stages on the path to hominization [p. 75 *n.* 1].

We can far more easily grasp another process of a later date. Under the influence of external factors into which we need not enter here and which are also in part insufficiently known, it came about that the matriarchal social order was succeeded by the patriarchal one—which, of course, involved a revolution

[1] [Cf. pp. 25–6 above.]

[2] [Cf. a remark on this in *Totem and Taboo* (1912–13), *Standard Ed.*, **13**, 80 *n.*]

in the juridical conditions that had so far prevailed. An echo of this revolution seems still to be audible in the *Oresteia* of Aeschylus.[1] But this turning from the mother to the father points in addition to a victory of intellectuality over sensuality—that is, an advance in civilization, since maternity is proved by the evidence of the senses while paternity is a hypothesis, based on an inference and a premiss. Taking sides in this way with a thought-process in preference to a sense perception has proved to be a momentous step.

At some point between the two events that I have mentioned[2] there was another which shows the most affinity to what we are investigating in the history of religion. Human beings found themselves obliged in general to recognise 'intellectual [*geistige*]' forces—forces, that is, which cannot be grasped by the senses (particularly by the sight) but which none the less produce undoubted and indeed extremely powerful effects. If we may rely upon the evidence of language, it was movement of the air that provided the prototype of intellectuality [*Geistigkeit*], for intellect [*Geist*] derives its name from a breath of wind—'*animus*', '*spiritus*',[3] and the Hebrew '*ruach* (breath)'. This too led to the discovery of the mind [*Seele* (soul)] as that of the intellectual [*geistigen*] principle in individual human beings. Observation found the movement of air once again in men's breathing, which ceases when they die. To this day a dying man 'breathes out his spirit [*Seele*]'. Now, however, the world of spirits [*Geisterreich*] lay open to men. They were prepared to attribute the soul [*Seele*] which they had discovered in themselves to everything in Nature. The whole world was animate [*beseelt*]; and science, which came so much later, had plenty to do in divesting part of the world of its soul once more; indeed it has not completed that task even to-day.[4]

The Mosaic prohibition elevated God to a higher degree of

[1] [The theme of this trilogy is the murder of Agamemnon by his wife Clytemnestra, the vengeance taken on her by their son Orestes, his pursuit by the Furies and his trial and acquittal by the Court of the Areopagus in Athens.]

[2] [Between the development of speech and the end of the matriarchy.]

[3] [In the original version of this Section (see p. 111 *n.*) the Greek word 'ἄνεμος (anemos, wind)' appears here as well.]

[4] [It will have been seen that this last paragraph is untranslatable. '*Geist*' means not only 'intellect' but 'spirit' and 'soul'. '*Seele*' means 'soul', 'spirit' and 'mind'.]

intellectuality, and the way was opened to further alterations in the idea of God which we have still to describe. But we may first consider another effect of the prohibition. All such advances in intellectuality have as their consequence that the individual's self-esteem is increased, that he is made proud—so that he feels superior to other people who have remained under the spell of sensuality. Moses, as we know, conveyed to the Jews an exalted sense of being a chosen people. The dematerialization of God brought a fresh and valuable contribution to their secret treasure. The Jews retained their inclination to intellectual interests. The nation's political misfortune taught it to value at its true worth the one possession that remained to it—its literature. Immediately after the destruction of the Temple in Jerusalem by Titus, the Rabbi Jochanan ben Zakkai asked permission to open the first Torah school in Jabneh.[1] From that time on, the Holy Writ and intellectual concern with it were what held the scattered people together.

This much is generally known and accepted. All I have wanted to do is to add that this characteristic development of the Jewish nature was introduced by the Mosaic prohibition against worshipping God in a visible form.

The pre-eminence given to intellectual labours throughout some two thousand years in the life of the Jewish people has, of course, had its effect. It has helped to check the brutality and the tendency to violence which are apt to appear where the development of muscular strength is the popular ideal. Harmony in the cultivation of intellectual and physical activity, such as was achieved by the Greek people, was denied to the Jews. In this dichotomy their decision was at least in favour of the worthier alternative.[2]

[1] [He is reputed to have escaped from Jerusalem in a coffin, and to have obtained leave from the Roman general to start a college for instruction in the Law (*Torah*) at a town near the sea to the west of Jerusalem (A.D. 70).]

[2] [In the original version (see p. 111 *n.*): 'the alternative that was more significant culturally.']

D

Renunciation of Instinct

It is not obvious and not immediately understandable why an advance in intellectuality, a set-back to sensuality, should raise the self-regard both of an individual and of a people. It seems to presuppose the existence of a definite standard of value and of some other person or agency which maintains it. For an explanation let us turn to an analogous case in individual psychology which we have come to understand.

If the id in a human being gives rise to an instinctual demand of an erotic or aggressive nature, the simplest and most natural thing is that the ego, which has the apparatus of thought and the muscular apparatus at its disposal, should satisfy the demand by an action. This satisfaction of the instinct is felt by the ego as pleasure, just as its non-satisfaction would undoubtedly have become a source of unpleasure. Now a case may arise in which the ego abstains from satisfying the instinct in view of external obstacles—namely, if it perceives that the action in question would provoke a serious danger to the ego. An abstention from satisfaction of this kind, the renunciation of an instinct on account of an external hindrance—or, as we say, in obedience to the reality principle—is not pleasurable in any event. The renunciation of the instinct would lead to a lasting tension owing to unpleasure, if it were not possible to reduce the strength of the instinct itself by displacements of energy. Instinctual renunciation can, however, also be imposed for other reasons, which we correctly describe as *internal*. In the course of an individual's development a portion of the inhibiting forces in the external world are internalized and an agency is constructed in the ego which confronts the rest of the ego in an observing, criticizing and prohibiting sense. We call this new agency the *super-ego*. Thenceforward the ego, before putting to work the instinctual satisfactions demanded by the id, has to take into account not merely the dangers of the external world but also the objections of the super-ego, and it will have all the more grounds for abstaining from satisfying the instinct. But whereas instinctual renunciation, when it is for external reasons, is *only* unpleasurable, when it is for internal reasons, in obedience to the super-ego, it has a different economic effect. In addition to the inevitable unpleasurable consequences it also brings the ego a yield of pleasure—a substitutive satisfaction, as it were. The ego feels elevated; it is proud of the instinctual renunciation, as though it were a valuable achievement. We believe we can understand the mechanism of this yield of pleasure. The super-ego is the successor and representative of the individual's parents (and educators) who had supervised his actions in the first period of his life; it carries on their functions almost unchanged. It keeps the ego in a permanent state of dependence and exercises a constant pressure on it. Just as in childhood, the ego is apprehensive about risking the love of its supreme master; it feels his approval as liberation and satisfaction and his reproaches as pangs of conscience. When the ego has brought the super-ego the sacrifice of an instinctual renunciation, it expects to be rewarded by receiving more love from it. The consciousness of deserving this love is felt by it as pride. At the time when the authority had not yet been internalized as a super-ego, there could be the same relation between the threat of loss of love and the claims of instinct: there was a feeling of security and satisfaction when one had achieved an instinctual renunciation out of love for one's parents. But this happy feeling could only assume the peculiar narcissistic character of pride after the authority had itself become a portion of the ego.

What help does this explanation of the satisfaction arising from instinctual renunciation give us towards understanding the processes that we want to study—the elevation of self-regard when there are advances in intellectuality? Very little, it seems. The circumstances are quite different. There is no question of any instinctual renunciation and there is no second person or agency for whose sake the sacrifice is made. We shall soon feel doubts about this last assertion. It can be said that the great man is precisely the authority for whose sake the achievement is carried out; and, since the great man himself operates by virtue of his similarity to the father, there is no need to feel surprise if in group psychology the role of the super-ego falls to him. So that this would apply too to the man Moses in relation to the Jewish people. As regards the other point, however, no proper analogy can be established. An advance in intellectuality consists in deciding against direct sense-perception in favour of what are known as the higher intellectual processes—that is, memories, reflections and inferences. It consists, for instance, in deciding that paternity is more important than maternity, although it cannot, like the latter, be established by the evidence of the senses, and that for that reason the child should bear his father's name and be his heir. Or it declares that our God is the greatest and mightiest, although he is invisible like a gale of wind or like the soul. The rejection of a sexual or aggressive instinctual demand seems to be something quite different from this. Moreover, in the case of some advances in intellectuality—for instance, in the case of the victory of patriarchy—we cannot point to the authority which lays down the standard which is to be regarded as higher. It cannot in this case be the father, since he is only elevated into being an authority by the advance itself. Thus we are faced by the phenomenon that in the course of the development of humanity sensuality is gradually overpowered by intellectuality and that men feel proud and exalted by every such advance. But we are unable to say why this should be so. It further happens later on that intellectuality itself is overpowered by the very puzzling emotional phenomenon of faith. Here we have the celebrated '*credo quia absurdum*',[1] and, once more, anyone who has succeeded in this regards it as a supreme achievement. Perhaps the common element in all these psychological situations is something else. Perhaps men simply pronounce that what is more difficult is higher, and their pride is merely their narcissism augmented by the consciousness of a difficulty overcome.

These are certainly not very fruitful considerations, and it might be thought that they have nothing at all to do with our enquiry as to what has determined the character of the Jewish people. That would only be to our advantage; but a certain connection with our problem is betrayed nevertheless by a fact which will concern us still more later on. The religion which began with the prohibition against making an image of God develops more and more in the course of centuries into a religion of instinctual renunciations. It is not that it would demand sexual *abstinence*; it is content with a marked restriction of sexual freedom. God, however, becomes entirely removed from sexuality and elevated into the ideal of ethical perfection. But ethics is a limitation of instinct. The Prophets are never tired of asseverating that God requires nothing other from his

[1] [See footnote 1, p. 85 above.]

people than a just and virtuous conduct of life—that is, abstention from every instinctual satisfaction which is still condemned as vicious by our morality to-day as well. And even the demand for belief in him seems to take a second place in comparison with the seriousness of these ethical requirements. In this way instinctual renunciation seems to play a prominent part in the religion, even if it did not stand out in it from the first.

This is the place, however, for an interpolation, in order to avoid a misunderstanding. Even though it may seem that instinctual renunciation and the ethics founded on it do not form part of the essential content of religion, yet genetically they are most intimately connected with it. Totemism,[1] which is the earliest form of a religion which we recognize, carries with it, as indispensable constituents of its system, a number of commands and prohibitions which have no other significance, of course, than as instinctual renunciations: the worship of the totem, which includes a prohibition against injuring or killing it, exogamy—that is, renunciation of the passionately desired mothers and sisters in the horde—the granting of equal rights to all the members of the fraternal alliance—that is, restricting the inclination to violent rivalry among them. In these regulations are to be seen the first beginnings of a moral and social order. It does not escape us that two different motives are at work here. The first two prohibitions operate on the side of the father who has been got rid of: they carry on his will, as it were. The third command—the granting of equal rights to the allied brothers—disregards the father's will; it is justified by an appeal to the necessity for permanently maintaining the new order which succeeded the father's removal. Otherwise a relapse into the earlier state would have become inevitable. It is here that social commands diverge from the others which, as we might say, are derived directly from religious connections.

The essential part of this course of events is repeated in the abbreviated development of the human individual. Here, too, it is the authority of the child's parents—essentially, that of his autocratic father, threatening him with his power to punish—which calls on him for a renunciation of instinct and which decides for him what is to be allowed and what forbidden. Later on, when Society and the super-ego have taken the parents' place, what in the child was called 'well-behaved' or

[1] [Cf. above p. 81 ff.]

'naughty' is described as 'good' and 'evil' or 'virtuous' and 'vicious'. But it is still always the same thing—instinctual renunciation under the pressure of the authority which replaces and prolongs the father.

A further depth is added to these discoveries when we examine the remarkable concept of holiness. What is it really that seems to us 'holy' in preference to other things that we value highly and recognize as important?[1] On the one hand, the connection of holiness or sacredness with what is religious is unmistakable. It is insisted upon emphatically: everything religious is sacred, it is the very core of sacredness. On the other hand, our judgement is disturbed by the numerous attempts to apply the characteristic of sacredness to so many other things—people, institutions, functions—which have little to do with religion. These efforts serve obvious tendentious purposes. Let us start from the prohibitive character which is so firmly attached to sacredness. What is sacred is obviously something that may not be touched. A sacred prohibition has a very strong emotional tone but has in fact no rational basis. For why, for instance, should incest with a daughter or sister be such a specially serious crime—so much worse than any other sexual intercourse?[2] If we ask for a rational basis we shall certainly be told that all our feelings rebel against it. But that only means that people regard the prohibition as self-evident and that they know of no basis for it.

It is easy enough to show the futility of such an explanation. What is represented as insulting our most sacred feelings was a universal custom—we might call it a usage made holy—among the ruling families of the Ancient Egyptians and of other early peoples. It was taken as a matter of course that a Pharaoh

[1] [The word '*heilig*', here translated either 'sacred' or 'holy', was discussed by Freud somewhat differently in his paper on ' "Civilized" Sexual Morality and Modern Nervous Illness' (1908*d*), *Standard Ed.*, **9**, 186–7. The gist of this latter argument is already to be seen in a remarkable short paragraph headed 'Definition of "Holiness" ' in a communication sent by Freud to Fliess on May 31st, 1897 (Freud, 1950*a*, Draft N). The word '*heilig*' appears also, as applied to *persons* in the sense of 'saintly', in Chapter VII of *Civilization and its Discontents* (1930*a*), *Standard Ed.*, **21**, 126. The wider aspects of the present topic are also considered in the same chapter. See especially, ibid., 125–30.]

[2] [The 'horror of incest' is the subject of the first Essay in *Totem and Taboo*, (1912–13). It, too, appears in Draft N (cf. the last footnote).]

should take his sister as his first and principal wife; and the later successors of the Pharaohs, the Greek Ptolemies, did not hesitate to follow that model. We are compelled, rather, to a realization that incest—in this instance between a brother and sister—was a privilege which was withheld from common mortals and reserved to kings as representatives of the gods, just as similarly, no objection was taken to incestuous relations of this kind in the world of Greek and Germanic legend. It may be suspected that the scrupulous insistence upon equality of birth among our aristocracy is a relic of this ancient privilege and it can be established that, as a result of the inbreeding practised over so many generations in the highest social strata, Europe is ruled to-day by members of a single family and a second one.

Evidence of incest among gods, kings and heroes helps us as well to deal with another attempt, which seeks to explain the horror of incest biologically and to trace it to an obscure knowledge of the damage done by inbreeding. It is not even certain, however, that there *is* any danger of damage from inbreeding—let alone that primitive peoples can have recognized it and reacted against it. The uncertainty in defining the permitted and forbidden degrees of kinship argues just as little in favour of the hypothesis that a 'natural feeling' is the ultimate basis of the horror of incest.

Our construction of prehistory forces us to another explanation. The command in favour of exogamy, of which the horror of incest is the negative expression, was a product of the will of the father and carried this will on after he had been removed. Hence come the strength of its emotional tone and the impossibility of finding a rational basis for it—that is, its sacredness. We confidently expect that an investigation of all the other cases of a sacred prohibition would lead to the same conclusion as in that of the horror of incest: that what is sacred was originally nothing other than the prolongation of the will of the primal father. This would also throw light on the hitherto incomprehensible ambivalence of the words which express the concept of sacredness. It is the ambivalence which in general dominates the relation to the father. [The Latin] '*sacer*' means not only 'sacred', 'consecrated', but also something that we can only translate as 'infamous', 'detestable' (e.g. '*auri sacra fames*').[1]

[1] ['Execrable hunger for gold.' Virgil, *Aeneid*, III, 57. Cf. 'The Antithetical Meaning of Primal Words' (1910*e*), *Standard Ed.*, **11**, 159.]

But the father's will was not only something which one might not touch, which one had to hold in high respect, but also something one trembled before, because it demanded a painful instinctual renunciation. When we hear that Moses made his people holy [p. 30] by introducing the custom of circumcision we now understand the deep meaning of that assertion. Circumcision is the symbolic substitute for the castration which the primal father once inflicted upon his sons in the plenitude of his absolute power, and whoever accepted that symbol was showing by it that he was prepared to submit to the father's will, even if it imposed the most painful sacrifice on him.

Going back to ethics, we may say in conclusion that a part of its precepts are justified rationally by the necessity for delimiting the rights of society as against the individual, the rights of the individual as against society and those of individuals as against one another. But what seems to us so grandiose about ethics, so mysterious and, in a mystical fashion, so self-evident, owes these characteristics to its connection with religion, its origin from the will of the father.

E

What is True in Religion

How enviable, to those of us who are poor in faith, do those enquirers seem who are convinced of the existence of a Supreme Being! To that great Spirit the world offers no problems, for he himself created all its institutions. How comprehensive, how exhaustive and how definitive are the doctrines of believers compared with the laborious, paltry and fragmentary attempts at explanation which are the most we are able to achieve! The divine Spirit, which is itself the ideal of ethical perfection, has planted in men the knowledge of that ideal and, at the same time, the urge to assimilate their own nature to it. They perceive directly what is higher and nobler and what is lower and more base. Their affective life is regulated in accordance with their distance from the ideal at any moment. When they approach to it—at their perihelion, as it were—they are brought high satisfaction; when, at their aphelion, they have become remote from it, the punishment is severe unpleasure. All of this is laid down so simply and so unshakably. We can only regret that certain experiences in life and observations in the world make it impossible for us to accept the premiss of the existence of such a Supreme Being. As though the world had not riddles enough, we are set the new problem of understanding how these other people have been able to acquire their belief in the Divine Being and whence that belief obtained its immense power, which overwhelms 'reason and science'.[1]

Let us return to the more modest problem which has occupied us hitherto. We wanted to explain the origin of the special character of the Jewish people, a character which is probably what has made their survival to the present day possible. We found that the man Moses impressed this character on them by giving them a religion which increased their self-esteem so much that they thought themselves superior to all other peoples. Thereafter they survived by keeping apart from others. Mixtures of blood interfered little with this, since what held them together was an ideal factor, the possession in common of certain intellectual and emotional wealth. The religion of Moses led to this result because (1) it allowed the people to take a share in the grandeur of a new idea of God, (2) it asserted that this people had been chosen by this great God and were destined to receive evidences of his special favour and (3) it forced upon the people an advance in intellectuality which, important enough in itself, opened the way, in addition, to the appreciation of intellectual work and to further renunciations of instinct.

This is what we have arrived at. And, though we do not wish to take back any of it, we cannot hide from ourselves that it is somehow or other unsatisfying. The cause does not, so to speak, match the effect; the fact that we want to explain seems to be of a different order of magnitude from everything by which we explain it. May it be that all the investigations we have so far made have not uncovered the whole of the motivation but only a certain superficial layer, and that behind it another very important factor awaits discovery? In view of the extraordinary complexity of all causation in life and history, something of the sort was to be expected.

Access to this deeper motivation would seem to be given at a

[1] [An allusion to an ironical remark by Mephistopheles in *Faust*, Part I, Scene 4.]

particular point in the previous discussions. The religion of Moses did not produce its effects immediately but in a remarkably indirect manner. This does not mean to say simply that it did not work at once, that it took long periods of time, hundreds of years, to deploy its full effect, for that is self-evident when it is a question of the imprinting of a people's character. But the restriction relates to a fact which we have derived from the history of the Jewish religion or, if you like, have introduced into it. We have said that after a certain time the Jewish people rejected the religion of Moses once more—whether they did so completely or retained some of its precepts we cannot guess. If we suppose that in the long period of the seizure of Canaan and the struggle with the peoples inhabiting it the Yahweh religion did not differ essentially from the worship of the other Baalim [p. 69], we shall be on historical ground in spite of all the later tendentious efforts to throw a veil over this shaming state of things.

The religion of Moses, however, had not disappeared without leaving a trace. A kind of memory of it had survived, obscured and distorted, supported, perhaps, among individual members of the priestly caste by ancient records. And it was this tradition of a great past which continued to work in the background, as it were, which gradually gained more and more power over men's minds, and which finally succeeded in transforming the god Yahweh into the god of Moses and in calling back to life the religion of Moses which had been established and then abandoned long centuries earlier.

In a previous portion of this essay [Sections C, D and E of Part I, p. 72 ff.] we have considered what assumption seems inevitable if we are to find such an achievement of tradition comprehensible.

F

The Return of the Repressed

There are a quantity of similar processes among those which the analytic investigation of mental life has taught us to know. Some of them are described as pathological, others are counted among the diversity of normal events. But that matters little, since the boundaries between the two [the pathological and the normal] are not sharply drawn, their mechanisms are to a large extent the same, and it is of far more importance whether the alterations in question take place in the ego itself or whether they confront it as alien to it—in which case they are known as symptoms.

From the mass of material I shall first bring forward some cases which relate to the development of character. Take, for instance, the girl who has reached a state of the most decided opposition to her mother. She has cultivated all those characteristics which she has seen that her mother lacked, and has avoided everything that reminded her of her mother. We may supplement this by saying that in her early years, like every female child, she adopted an identification with her mother and that she is now rebelling against this energetically. But when this girl marries and herself becomes a wife and a mother, we need not be surprised to find that she begins to grow more and more like the mother to whom she was so antagonistic, till finally the identification with her which she surmounted is unmistakably re-established. The same thing happens too with boys; and even the great Goethe, who in the period of his genius certainly looked down upon his unbending and pedantic father, in his old age developed traits which formed a part of his father's character. The outcome can become even more striking when the contrast between the two personalities is sharper. A young man whose fate it was to grow up beside a worthless father, began by developing, in defiance of him, into a capable, trustworthy and honourable person. In the prime of life his character was reversed, and thenceforward he behaved as though he had taken this same father as a model. In order not to miss the connection with our theme, we must keep in mind the fact that at the beginning of such a course of events there is always an identification with the father in early childhood. This is afterwards repudiated, and even overcompensated, but in the end establishes itself once more.

It has long since become common knowledge that the experiences of a person's first five years exercise a determining effect on his life, which nothing later can withstand. Much that deserves knowing might be said about the way in which these early impressions maintain themselves against any influences in more mature periods of life—but it would not be relevant here.

It may, however, be less well known that the strongest compulsive influence arises from impressions which impinge upon a child at a time when we would have to regard his psychical apparatus as not yet completely receptive. The fact itself cannot be doubted; but it is so puzzling that we may make it more comprehensible by comparing it with a photographic exposure which can be developed after any interval of time and transformed into a picture. I am nevertheless glad to point out that this uncomfortable discovery of ours has been anticipated by an imaginative writer, with the boldness that is permitted to poets. E. T. A. Hoffmann used to trace back the wealth of figures that put themselves at his disposal for his creative writings to the changing images and impressions which he had experienced during a journey of some weeks in a post-chaise while he was still an infant at his mother's breast.[1] What children have experienced at the age of two and have not understood, need never be remembered by them except in dreams; they may only come to know of it through psycho-analytic treatment. But at some later time it will break into their life with obsessional impulses, it will govern their actions, it will decide their sympathies and antipathies and will quite often determine their choice of a love-object, for which it is so frequently impossible to find a rational basis. The two points at which these facts touch upon our problem cannot be mistaken.

First, there is the remoteness of the period concerned,[2] which is recognized here as the truly determining factor—in the special state of the memory, for instance, which in the case of these childhood experiences we classify as 'unconscious'. We expect to find an analogy in this with the state which we are seeking to attribute to tradition in the mental life of the people. It was not easy, to be sure, to introduce the idea of the unconscious into group psychology.

Regular contributions [secondly] are made to the phenomena we are in search of by the mechanisms which lead to the formation of neuroses. Here again the determining events occur

[1] [The source of this reference has not been discovered.]

[2] Here, too, a poet may speak. In order to explain his attachment, he imagines: 'Ach, du warst in abgelebten Zeiten meine Schwester oder meine Frau.' [Literally: 'Ah, you were, in a past life, my sister or my wife.' From a poem dedicated by Goethe to Charlotte von Stein: 'Warum gabst du uns die tiefen Blicke.' Freud had quoted it in his Goethe House address (1930*e*), *Standard Ed.*, **21**, 209.]

in early childhood times, but here the stress is not upon the *time* but upon the process by which the event is met, the reaction to it. We can describe it schematically thus. As a result of the experience, an instinctual demand arises which calls for satisfaction. The ego refuses that satisfaction, either because it is paralysed by the magnitude of the demand or because it recognizes it as a danger. The former of these grounds is the more primary one; both of them amount to the avoidance of a situation of danger.[1] The ego fends off the danger by the process of repression. The instinctual impulse is in some way inhibited, its precipitating cause, with its attendant perceptions and ideas, is forgotten. This, however, is not the end of the process: the instinct has either retained its forces, or collects them again, or it is reawakened by some new precipitating cause. Thereupon it renews its demand, and, since the path to normal satisfaction remains closed to it by what we may call the scar of repression, somewhere, at a weak spot, it opens another path for itself to what is known as a substitutive satisfaction, which comes to light as a symptom, without the acquiescence of the ego, but also without its understanding. All the phenomena of the formation of symptoms may justly be described as the 'return of the repressed'.[2] Their distinguishing characteristic, however, is the far-reaching distortion to which the returning material has been subjected as compared with the original. It will perhaps be thought that this last group of facts has carried us too far away from the similarity with tradition. But we ought not to regret it if it has brought us close to the problems of the renunciation of instinct.

G

Historical Truth

We have undertaken all these psychological diversions in order to make it more credible to us that the religion of Moses only carried through its effect on the Jewish people as a

[1] [For 'situations of danger' see Addendum B in Chapter XI of *Inhibitions, Symptoms and Anxiety* (1926*d*), *Standard Ed.*, **20**, 164 ff.]

[2] [The term, as well as the concept, go back at least to Freud's second paper on the neuro-psychoses of defence (1896*b*), *Standard Ed.*, **3**, 170.]

tradition. It is likely that we have not achieved more than a certain degree of probability. Let us suppose, however, that we have succeeded in completely proving it. Even so the impression would remain that we have merely satisfied the *qualitative* factor of what was demanded, but not the quantitative one as well. There is an element of grandeur about everything to do with the origin of a religion, certainly including the Jewish one, and this is not matched by the explanations we have hitherto given. Some other factor must be involved to which there is little that is analogous and nothing that is of the same kind, something unique and something of the same order of magnitude as what has come out of it, as religion itself. [Cf. p. 123 above.]

Let us try to approach the subject from the opposite direction. We understand how a primitive man is in need of a god as creator of the universe, as chief of his clan, as personal protector. This god takes his position behind the dead fathers [of the clan], about whom tradition still has something to say. A man of later days, of our own day, behaves in the same way. He, too, remains childish and in need of protection, even when he is grown up; he thinks he cannot do without support from his god. That much is undisputed. But it is less easy to understand why there may only be a *single* god, why precisely the advance from henotheism[1] to monotheism acquires an overwhelming significance. No doubt it is true, as we have explained [pp. 106 and 123], that the believer has a share in the greatness of his god; and the greater the god the more reliable is the protection which he can offer. But a god's power does not necessarily presuppose that he is the only one. Many peoples regarded it only as a glorification of their chief god if he ruled over other deities who were inferior to him, and they did not think it diminished his greatness if there were other gods besides him. No doubt, if this god became a universal one and had all countries and peoples as his concern, it meant a sacrifice of intimacy, too. It was as though one were sharing one's god with the foreigners and one had to make up for this by the proviso that one was preferred by him. We can make the further point that the idea of a single

[1] [The word has not been very clearly defined. It is used to mean the belief of a community in one particular god of its own, and also to mean the belief in the dominance of one particular god over a hierarchy of other gods. In neither case does the belief imply that the god in question is the *only* god.]

god means in itself an advance in intellectuality, but it is impossible to rate this point so highly.

Pious believers, however, know how to fill this obvious gap in motivation adequately. They say that the idea of a single god produced such an overwhelming effect on men because it is a portion of the eternal *truth* which, long concealed, came to light at last and was then bound to carry everyone along with it. We must admit that a factor of this kind is at last something that matches the magnitude both of the subject and of its effect.

We too would like to accept this solution. But we are brought up by a doubt. The pious argument rests on an optimistic and idealistic premiss. It has not been possible to demonstrate in other connections that the human intellect has a particularly fine flair for the truth or that the human mind shows any special inclination for recognizing the truth. We have rather found, on the contrary, that our intellect very easily goes astray without any warning, and that nothing is more easily believed by us than what, without reference to the truth, comes to meet our wishful illusions. We must for that reason add a reservation to our agreement. We too believe that the pious solution contains the truth—but the *historical* truth and not the *material* truth. And we assume the right to correct a certain distortion to which this truth has been subjected on its return. That is to say, we do not believe that there is a single great god to-day, but that in primaeval times there was a single person who was bound to appear huge at that time and who afterwards returned in men's memory elevated to divinity.

We had assumed that the religion of Moses was to begin with rejected and half-forgotten and afterwards broke through as a tradition. We are now assuming that this process was being repeated then for the second time. When Moses brought the people the idea of a single god, it was not a novelty but signified the revival of an experience in the primaeval ages of the human family which had long vanished from men's conscious memory. But it had been so important and had produced or paved the way for such deeply penetrating changes in men's life that we cannot avoid believing that it had left behind it in the human mind some permanent traces, which can be compared to a tradition.

We have learnt from the psycho-analyses of individuals that

their earliest impressions, received at a time when the child was scarcely yet capable of speaking, produce at some time or another effects of a compulsive character without themselves being consciously remembered. We believe we have a right to make the same assumption about the earliest experiences of the whole of humanity. One of these effects would be the emergence of the idea of a single great god—an idea which must be recognized as a completely justified memory, though, it is true, one that has been distorted. An idea such as this has a compulsive character: it *must* be believed. To the extent to which it is distorted, it may be described as a *delusion*; in so far as it brings a return of the past, it must be called the *truth*. Psychiatric delusions, too, contain a small fragment of truth and the patient's conviction extends over from this truth on to its delusional wrappings.[1]

What follows, from here to the end, is a slightly modified repetition of the discussions in Part I [of the present (third) essay].

In 1912 I attempted, in my *Totem and Taboo*, to reconstruct the ancient situation from which these consequences followed. In doing so, I made use of some theoretical ideas put forward

[1] [The notion contained in this last sentence had been expressed by Freud in very similar terms in the first edition of *The Psychopathology of Everyday Life* (1901*b*), *Standard Ed.*, **6**, 256. Similarly in *Gradiva* (1907*a*), ibid., **9**, 80. The matter was investigated more deeply in Section B of the paper on 'Some Neurotic Mechanisms' (1922*b*), ibid., **18**, 225 ff.; but the general idea can be followed much further back—to the second paper on the neuro-psychoses of defence (1896*b*), ibid., **3**, 183 ff. and to passages in the Fliess correspondence dating from January 24, 1897 and January 1, 1896 (Freud, 1950*a*, Letter 57 and the section on paranoia in Draft K).—The related distinction drawn in this section between 'historical' and 'material' truth is of much more recent origin. There may be a hint of it in *The Future of an Illusion* (1927*c*), ibid., **21**, 44 and there is a more definite allusion to it in connection with myths in the paper on the acquisition of fire (1932*a*), ibid., **22**, 191. But the first explicit reference is in the 'Postscript' to the *Autobiographical Study* (1935*a*), ibid., **20**, 72, where the idea is mentioned as being already in existence, though in fact Freud did not express it in print again before 'Constructions in Analysis' (1937*d*), ibid., **23**, 267 ff. The subject has already been touched upon above, pp. 58 and 85.—For a reference to a possibly analogous distinction between psychical and external reality see p. 76 above.]

by Darwin, Atkinson and particularly by Robertson Smith, and combined them with the findings and indications derived from psycho-analysis. From Darwin I borrowed the hypothesis that human beings originally lived in small hordes, each of which was under the despotic rule of an older male who appropriated all the females and castigated or disposed of the younger males, including his sons. From Atkinson I took, in continuation of this account, the idea that this patriarchal system ended in a rebellion by the sons, who banded together against their father, overcame him and devoured him in common. Basing myself on Robertson Smith's totem theory, I assumed that subsequently the father-horde gave place to the totemic brother-clan. In order to be able to live in peace with one another, the victorious brothers renounced the women on whose account they had, after all, killed their father, and instituted exogamy. The power of fathers was broken and the families were organized as a matriarchy. The ambivalent emotional attitude of the sons to their father remained in force during the whole of later development. A particular animal was set up in the father's place as a totem. It was regarded as ancestor and protective spirit and might not be injured or killed. But once a year the whole male community came together to a ceremonial meal at which the totem animal (worshipped at all other times) was torn to pieces and devoured in common. No one might absent himself from this meal: it was the ceremonial repetition of the killing of the father, with which social order, moral laws and religion had taken their start. The conformity between Robertson Smith's totem meal and the Christian Lord's Supper had struck a number of writers before me. [See above, pp. 81–4.]

To this day I hold firmly to this construction. I have repeatedly met with violent reproaches for not having altered my opinions in later editions of my book in spite of the fact that more recent ethnologists have unanimously rejected Robertson Smith's hypotheses and have in part brought forward other, totally divergent theories. I may say in reply that these ostensible advances are well known to me. But I have not been convinced either of the correctness of these innovations or of Robertson Smith's errors. A denial is not a refutation, an innovation is not necessarily an advance. Above all, however, I am not an ethnologist but a psycho-analyst. I had a right to take out of ethnological literature what I might need for the work of analysis.

The writings of Robertson Smith—a man of genius—have given me valuable points of contact with the psychological material of analysis and indications for its employment. I have never found myself on common ground with his opponents.

H

The Historical Development

I cannot here repeat the contents of *Totem and Taboo* in greater detail. But I must undertake to fill up the long stretch between that hypothetical primaeval period and the victory of monotheism in historical times. After the institution of the combination of brother-clan, matriarchy, exogamy and totemism, a development began which must be described as a slow 'return of the repressed'. Here I am not using the term 'the repressed' in its proper sense. What is in question is something in a people's life which is past, lost to view, superseded and which we venture to compare with what is repressed in the mental life of an individual. We cannot at first sight say in what form this past existed during the time of its eclipse. It is not easy for us to carry over the concepts of individual psychology into group psychology; and I do not think we gain anything by introducing the concept of a 'collective' unconscious. The content of the unconscious, indeed, is in any case a collective, universal property of mankind. For the moment, then, we will make shift with the use of analogies. The processes in the life of peoples which we are studying here are very similar to those familiar to us in psychopathology, but nevertheless not quite the same. We must finally make up our minds to adopt the hypothesis that the psychical precipitates of the primaeval period became inherited property which, in each fresh generation, called not for acquisition but only for awakening. In this we have in mind the example of what is certainly the 'innate' symbolism which derives from the period of the development of speech, which is familiar to all children without their being instructed, and which is the same among all peoples despite their different languages. What we may perhaps still lack in certainty here is made good by other products of psycho-analytic research. We find that in a number of important relations our children react, not in a manner corresponding to their own experience, but instinctively, like the animals, in a manner that is only explicable as phylogenetic acquisition.[1]

The return of the repressed took place slowly and certainly not spontaneously but under the influence of all the changes in conditions of life which fill the history of human civilization. I cannot give a survey here of these determinants nor more than a fragmentary enumeration of the stages of this return. The father once more became the head of the family, but was not by any means so absolute as the father of the primal horde had been. The totem animal was replaced by a god in a series of transitions which are still very plain. To begin with, the god in human form still bore an animal's head; later he turned himself by preference into that particular animal, and afterwards it became sacred to him and was his favourite attendant; or he killed the animal and himself bore its name as an epithet. Between the totem animal and the god, the hero emerged, often as a preliminary step towards deification. The idea of a supreme deity seems to have started early, at first only in a shadowy manner without intruding into men's daily interests. As tribes and peoples came together into larger unities, the gods too organized themselves into families and into hierarchies. One of them was often elevated into being supreme lord over gods and men. After this, the further step was hesitatingly taken of paying respect to only one god, and finally the decision was taken of giving all power to a single god and of tolerating no other gods beside him. Only thus was it that the supremacy of the father of the primal horde was re-established and that the emotions relating to him could be repeated.

The first effect of meeting the being who had so long been missed and longed for was overwhelming and was like the traditional description of the law-giving from Mount Sinai. Admiration, awe and thankfulness for having found grace in his eyes—the religion of Moses knew none but these positive feelings towards the father-god. The conviction of his irresistibility, the submission to his will, could not have been more unquestioning in the helpless and intimidated son of the father of the horde—

[1] [What Freud has in mind here are no doubt chiefly the 'primal phantasies'. See the Editor's footnote on the 'archaic heritage' (p. 102 above). The word translated here 'instinctively' is '*instinktmässig*'. Cf. p. 100 above.]

indeed those feelings only become fully intelligible when they are transposed into the primitive and infantile setting. A child's emotional impulses are intensely and inexhaustibly deep to a degree quite other than those of an adult; only religious ecstasy can bring them back. A rapture of devotion to God was thus the first reaction to the return of the great father.

The direction to be taken by this father-religion was in this way laid down for all time. Yet this did not bring its development to an end. Ambivalence is a part of the essence of the relation to the father: in the course of time the hostility too could not fail to stir, which had once driven the sons into killing their admired and dreaded father. There was no place in the framework of the religion of Moses for a direct expression of the murderous hatred of the father. All that could come to light was a mighty reaction against it—a sense of guilt on account of that hostility, a bad conscience for having sinned against God and for not ceasing to sin. This sense of guilt, which was uninterruptedly kept awake by the Prophets, and which soon formed an essential part of the religious system, had yet another superficial motivation, which neatly disguised its true origin. Things were going badly for the people; the hopes resting on the favour of God failed in fulfilment; it was not easy to maintain the illusion, loved above all else, of being God's chosen people. If they wished to avoid renouncing that happiness, a sense of guilt on account of their own sinfulness offered a welcome means of exculpating God: they deserved no better than to be punished by him since they had not obeyed his commandments. And, driven by the need to satisfy this sense of guilt, which was insatiable and came from sources so much deeper, they must make those commandments grow ever stricter, more meticulous and even more trivial. In a fresh rapture of moral asceticism they imposed more and more new instinctual renunciations on themselves and in that way reached—in doctrine and precept, at least—ethical heights which had remained inaccessible to the other peoples of antiquity. Many Jews regard this attainment of ethical heights as the second main characteristic and the second great achievement of their religion. The way in which it was connected with the first one—the idea of a single god—should be plain from our remarks. These ethical ideas cannot, however, disavow their origin from the sense of guilt felt on account of a suppressed hostility to God. They possess the characteristic—uncompleted and incapable of completion—of obsessional neurotic reaction-formations; we can guess, too, that they serve the secret purposes of punishment.

The further development takes us beyond Judaism. The remainder of what returned from the tragic drama of the primal father was no longer reconcilable in any way with the religion of Moses. The sense of guilt of those days was very far from being any longer restricted to the Jewish people; it had caught hold of all the Mediterranean peoples as a dull *malaise*, a premonition of calamity for which no one could suggest a reason. Historians of our day speak of an ageing of ancient civilization, but I suspect that they have only grasped accidental and contributory causes of this depressed mood of the peoples. The elucidation of this situation of depression sprang from Jewry. Irrespectively of all the approximations and preparations in the surrounding world, it was after all a Jewish man, Saul of Tarsus (who, as a Roman citizen, called himself Paul), in whose spirit the realization first emerged: 'the reason we are so unhappy is that we have killed God the father.' And it is entirely understandable that he could only grasp this piece of truth in the delusional disguise of the glad tidings: 'we are freed from all guilt since one of us has sacrificed his life to absolve us.' In this formula the killing of God was of course not mentioned, but a crime that had to be atoned by the sacrifice of a victim could only have been a murder. And the intermediate step between the delusion and the historical truth was provided by the assurance that the victim of the sacrifice had been God's son. With the strength which it derived from the source of historical truth, this new faith overthrew every obstacle. The blissful sense of being chosen was replaced by the liberating sense of redemption. But the fact of the parricide, in returning to the memory of mankind, had to overcome greater resistances than the other fact, which had constituted the subject-matter of monotheism;[1] it was also obliged to submit to a more powerful distortion. The unnameable crime was replaced by the hypothesis of what must be described as a shadowy 'original sin'.

Original sin and redemption by the sacrifice of a victim became the foundation stones of the new religion founded by Paul. It must remain uncertain whether there was a ringleader

[1] [Namely, the fact of the existence of the primal father.]

and instigator to the murder among the band of brothers who rebelled against the primal father, or whether such a figure was created later by the imagination of creative artists in order to turn themselves into heroes, and was then introduced into the tradition. After the Christian doctrine had burst the framework of Judaism, it took up components from many other sources, renounced a number of characteristics of pure monotheism and adapted itself in many details to the rituals of the other Mediterranean peoples. It was as though Egypt was taking vengeance once more on the heirs of Akhenaten. It is worth noticing how the new religion dealt with the ancient ambivalence in the relation to the father. Its main content was, it is true, reconciliation with God the Father, atonement for the crime committed against him; but the other side of the emotional relation showed itself in the fact that the son, who had taken the atonement on himself, became a god himself beside the father and, actually, in place of the father. Christianity, having arisen out of a father-religion, became a son-religion. It has not escaped the fate of having to get rid of the father.

Only a portion of the Jewish people accepted the new doctrine. Those who refused to are still called Jews to-day. Owing to this cleavage, they have become even more sharply divided from other peoples than before. They were obliged to hear the new religious community (which, besides Jews, included Egyptians, Greeks, Syrians, Romans and eventually Germans) reproach them with having murdered God. In full, this reproach would run as follows: 'They will not accept it as true that they murdered God, whereas we admit it and have been cleansed of that guilt.' It is easy therefore to see how much truth lies behind this reproach. A special enquiry would be called for to discover why it has been impossible for the Jews to join in this forward step which was implied, in spite of all its distortions, by the admission of having murdered God. In a certain sense they have in that way taken a tragic load of guilt on themselves; they have been made to pay heavy penance for it.

Our investigation may perhaps have thrown a little light on the question of how the Jewish people have acquired the characteristics which distinguish them. Less light has been thrown on the problem of how it is that they have been able to retain their individuality till the present day. But exhaustive answers to such riddles cannot in fairness be either demanded or expected. A contribution, to be judged in view of the limitations which I mentioned at the start [p. 105], is all that I can offer.

BIBLIOGRAPHY AND AUTHOR INDEX

[Titles of books and periodicals are in italics; titles of papers are in inverted commas. Abbreviations are in accordance with the *World List of Scientific Periodicals* (London, 1952). Further abbreviations used in this volume will be found in the List at the end of this bibliography. Numerals in thick type refer to volumes; ordinary numerals refer to pages. The figures in round brackets at the end of each entry indicate the page or pages of this volume on which the work in question is mentioned. In the case of the Freud entries, the letters attached to the dates of publication are in accordance with the corresponding entries in the complete bibliography of Freud's writings to be included in the last volume of the *Standard Edition.*

For non-technical authors, and for technical authors where no specific work is mentioned, see the General Index.]

ATKINSON, J. J. (1903) *Primal Law*, London. Included in LANG, A., *Social Origins*, London, 1903. (81, 130–1)

AUERBACH, E. (1932, 1936) *Wüste und Gelobtes Land* (2 vols.), Berlin. (42, 43, 63)

BREASTED, J. H. (1906) *A History of Egypt*, London. (8, 21–3)

(1934) *The Dawn of Conscience*, London. (8–9, 21–4, 50)

BREUER, J. and FREUD, S. (1895) *See* FREUD, S. (1895*d*)

Cambridge Ancient History (1924) (ed. J. B. Bury, S. A. Cook and F. E. Adcock), Vol. II, *The Egyptian and Hittite Empires to* 1000 *B.C.*, Cambridge. (Historical Egyptian Chapters by J. H. Breasted.) (21)

DARWIN, C. (1871) *The Descent of Man* (2 vols.), London. (81, 130–1)

Encyclopaedia Britannica (1910), Eleventh Edition, Vol. III, Cambridge. (42)

ERMAN, A. (1905) *Die Ägyptische Religion*, Berlin. (22, 24, 30)

FRAZER, J. G. (1911) *The Dying God* (*The Golden Bough*, 3rd ed., Part III), London. (89, 110)

FREUD, S. (1895*d*) With BREUR, J., *Studien über Hysterie*, Vienna. *G.S.*, **1**, 3; *G.W.*, **1**, 77 (omitting Breuer's contributions). (107)
[*Trans.: Studies on Hysteria*, London, 1956; *Standard Ed.*, **2**; *I.P.L.*, **50** (including Breuer's contributions).]

(1896*b*) 'Weitere Bemerkungen über die Abwehr-Neuropsychosen', *G.S.*, **1**, 363; *G.W.*, **1**, 379. (127, 130)
[*Trans.:* 'Further Remarks on the Neuro-Psychoses of Defence', *C.P.*, **1**, 155; *Standard Ed.*, **3**, 159.]

(1900*a*) *Die Traumdeutung*, Vienna. *G.S.*, **2–3**; *G.W.*, **2–3**. (10, 12, 102)

FREUD, S. (*contd.*)
[*Trans.: The Interpretation of Dreams*, London and New York, 1955; *Standard Ed.*, **4–5**.]

(1901*b*) *Zur Psychopathologie des Alltagslebens*, Berlin, 1904. *G.S.*, **4**, 3; *G.W.*, **4.** (130)
[*Trans.: The Psychopathology of Everyday Life*, *Standard Ed.*, **6**.]

(1907*a*) *Der Wahn und die Träume in W. Jensens 'Gradiva'*, Vienna. *G.S.*, **9**, 273; *G.W.*, **7**, 31. (130)
[*Trans.: Delusions and Dreams in Jensen's 'Gradiva'*, *Standard Ed.*, **9**, 3.]

(1908*c*) 'Uber infantile Sexualtheorien', *G.S.*, **5**, 158; *G.W.*, **7**, 171. (74)
[*Trans.*: 'On the Sexual Theories of Children', *C.P.*, **2**, 59; *Standard Ed.*, **9**, 207.]

(1908*d*) 'Die "kulturelle" Sexualmoral und die moderne Nervosität', *G.S.*, **5**, 143; *G.W.*, **7**, 143. (120)
[*Trans.*: ' "Civilized" Sexual Morality and Modern Nervous Illness', *C.P.*, **2**, 76; *Standard Ed.*, **9**, 179.]

(1909*b*) 'Analyse der Phobie eines fünfjährigen Knaben', *G.S.*, **8**, 129; *G.W.*, **7**, 243. (92)
[*Trans.*: 'Analysis of a Phobia in a Five-Year-Old Boy', *C.P.*, **3**, 149; *Standard Ed.*, **10**, 3.]

(1909*c*) 'Der Familienroman der Neurotiker', *G.S.*, **12**, 367; *G.W.*, **7**, 227. (12)
[*Trans.*: 'Family Romances', *C.P.*, **5**, 74; *Standard Ed.*, **9**, 237.]

(1910*a* [1909]) *Über Psychoanalyse*, Vienna. *G.S.*, **4**, 349; *G.W.*, **8**, 3. (107)
[*Trans.*: 'Five Lectures on Psycho-Analysis', *Standard Ed.*, **11**, 3.]

(1910*c*) *Eine Kindheitserinnerung des Leonardo da Vinci*, Vienna. *G.S.*, **9**, 371; *G.W.* **8**, 128. (92)
[*Trans.: Leonardo da Vinci and a Memory of His Childhood*, *Standard Ed.*, **11**, 59.]

(1910*e*) ' "Über den Gegensinn der Urworte" ', *G.S.*, **10**, 221; *G.W.*, **8**, 214. (121)
[*Trans.*: ' "The Antithetical Meaning of Primal Words" ', *C.P.*, **4**, 184; *Standard Ed.*, **11**, 155.]

(1912–13) *Totem und Tabu*, Vienna. 1913. *G.S.*, **10**, 3; *G.W.*, **9**. (5, 53, 55, 58, 81–4, 102, 113, 120, 130–2)
[*Trans.: Totem and Taboo*, London, 1950; New York, 1952; *Standard Ed.*, **13**, 1.]

(1914*d*) 'Zur Geschichte der psychoanalytischen Bewegung', *G.S.*, **4**, 411; *G.W.*, **10**, 44. (73)
[*Trans.*: 'On the History of the Psycho-Analytic Movement', *C.P.*, **1**, 287; *Standard Ed.*, **14**, 3.]

(1914*g*) 'Weitere Ratschläge zur Technik der Psychoanalyse:

II. Erinnern, Wiederholen und Durcharbeiten', *G.S.*, **6,** 109; *G.W.*, **10,** 126. (89)
[*Trans.:* 'Remembering, Repeating and Working-Through (Further Recommendations on the Technique of Psycho-Analysis, II)', *C.P.*, **2,** 366; *Standard Ed.*, **12,** 147.]

(1915*c*) 'Triebe und Triebschicksale', *G.S.*, **5,** 443; *G.W.*, **10,** 210. (102)
[*Trans.:* 'Instincts and their Vicissitudes', *C.P.*, **4,** 60; *Standard Ed.*, **14,** 111.]

(1915*e*) 'Das Unbewusste', *G.S.*, **5,** 480; *G.W.*, **10,** 264. (97)
[*Trans.:* 'The Unconscious', *C.P.*, **4,** 98; *Standard Ed.*, **14,** 161.]

(1916–17) *Vorlesungen zur Einführung in die Psychoanalyse* ,Vienna. *G.S.*, **7**; *G.W.*, **11.** (9, 73, 74, 102, 104)
[*Trans.:* *Introductory Lectures on Psycho-Analysis*, revised ed., New York, 1966; London, 1971; *Standard Ed.*, **15–16.**]

(1918*b* [1914]) 'Aus der Geschichte einer infantilen Neurose', *G.S.*, **8,** 439; *G.W.*, **12,** 29. (102)
[*Trans.:* 'From the History of an Infantile Neurosis', *C.P.*, **3,** 473; *Standard Ed.*, **17,** 3.]

(1919*e*) ' "Ein Kind wird geschlagen" ', *G.S.*, **5,** 344; *G.W.*, **12,** 197. (102)
[*Trans.:* ' "A Child is Being Beaten" ', *C.P.*, **2,** 172; *Standard Ed.*, **17,** 177.]

(1919*g*) Preface to Reik *Probleme der Religionspsychologie*, Vienna. *G.S.*, **11,** 256; *G.W.*, **12,** 325. (102)
[*Trans.:* In T. Reik's *Ritual: Psycho-Analytic Studies*, London and New York, 1931. *C.P.*, **5,** 92; *Standard Ed.*, **17,** 259.]

(1920*g*) *Jenseits des Lustprinzips*, Vienna. *G.S.*, **6,** 191; *G.W.*, **13,** 3. (97)
[*Trans.:* *Beyond the Pleasure Principle*, London, 1961; *Standard Ed.*, **18,** 7; *I.P.L.*, **4.**]

(1921*c*) *Massenpsychologie und Ich-Analyse*, Vienna. *G.S.*, **6,** 261; *G.W.*, **13,** 73. (5, 84)
[*Trans.:* *Group Psychology and the Analysis of the Ego*, London and New York, 1959; *Standard Ed.*, **18,** 69; *I.P.L.*, **6.**]

(1922*b*) 'Über einige neurotische Mechanismen bei Eifersucht, Paranoia und Homosexualität', *G.S.*, **5,** 387; *G.W.*, **13,** 195. (130)
[*Trans.:* 'Some Neurotic Mechanisms in Jealousy, Paranoia and Homosexuality', *C.P.*, **2,** 232; *Standard Ed.*, **18,** 223.]

(1923*b*) *Das Ich und das Es*, Vienna. *G.S.*, **6,** 353; *G.W.*, **13,** 237. (78, 95, 97, 102)
[*Trans.:* *The Ego and the Id*, London and New York, 1962; *Standard Ed*, **19,** 3; *I.PL.*, **12.**]

(1925*d* [1924]) *Selbstdarstellung*, Vienna, 1934. *G.S.*, **11,** 119; *G.W.*, **14,** 33. (90)
[*Trans.:* *An Autobiographical Study*, London, 1935 (*Auto-*

FREUD, S. (*contd.*)
biography, New York, 1935); *Standard Ed.*, **20,** 3.]
(1926*d*) *Hemmung, Symptom und Angst*, Vienna. *G.S.*, **11,** 23; *G.W.*, **14,** 113. (127)
[*Trans.: Inhibitions, Symptoms and Anxiety*, London, 1960 (*The Problem of Anxiety*, New York, 1936); *Standard Ed.*, **20,** 77; *I.P.L.*, **28**.]
(1927*c*) *Die Zukunft einer Illusion*, Vienna. *G.S.*, **11,** 411; *G.W.*, **14,** 325. (85, 130)
[*Trans.: The Future of an Illusion*, London, 1962; New York 1928; *Standard Ed.*, **21,** 3; *I.P.L.*, **15**.]
(1930*a*) *Das Unbehagen in der Kultur*, Vienna. *G.S.*, **12,** 29; *G.W.*, **14,** 421. (91, 92, 120)
[*Trans.: Civilization and its Discontents*, New York, 1961; London, 1963; *Standard Ed.*, **21,** 59; *I.P.L.*, **17**.]
(1930*e*) Ansprache im Frankfurter Goethe-Haus, *G.S.*, **12,** 408; *G.W.*, **14,** 547. (126)
[*Trans.:* Address delivered in the Goethe House at Frankfurt, *Standard Ed.*, **21,** 208.]
(1932*a*) 'Zur Gewinnung des Feuers', *G.S.*, **12,** 141; *G.W.*, **16,** 3. (130)
[*Trans.:* 'The Acquisition and Control of Fire', *C.P.*, **5,** 288; *Standard Ed.*, **22,** 185.]
(1933*a*) *Neue Folge der Vorlesungen zur Einführung in die Psychoanalyse*, Vienna. *G.S.*, **12,** 151; *G.W.*, **15,** (95, 97)
[*Trans.: New Introductory Lectures on Psycho-Analysis*, New York, 1966; London, 1971; *Standard Ed.*, **22,** 3; *I.P.L.*, **24**.]
(1935*a*) Postscript (1935) to *An Autobiographical Study*, new edition, London and New York; *Standard Ed.*, **20,** 71. (130)
[*German Text:* 'Nachschrift 1935 zur *Selbstdarstellung*', 2nd edition, Vienna, 1936; *G.W.*, **16,** 31. German original first appeared late in 1935.]
(1937*b*) 'Moses ein Ägypter', *G.W.*, **16,** 103, (3–4)
[*Trans.:* 'Moses an Egyptian', Part I of *Moses and Monotheism* (1939*a*); *Standard Ed.*, **23,** 7; *I.P.L.*, **33,** 7.]
(1937*c*) 'Die endliche und die unendliche Analyse', *G.W.*, **16,** 59. (77, 102)
[*Trans.:* 'Analysis Terminable and Interminable', *C.P.*, **5,** 316; *Standard Ed.*, **23,** 211.]
(1937*d*) 'Konstruktionen in der Analyse', *G.W.*, **16,** 43. (130)
[*Trans.:* 'Constructions in Analysis', *C.P.*, **5,** 358; *Standard Ed.*, **23,** 257.]
(1937*e*) 'Wenn Moses ein Ägypter war . . .', *G.W.*, **16,** 114. (3–4)
[*Trans.:* 'If Moses was an Egyptian . . .', Part II of *Moses and Monotheism* (1939*a*); *Standard Ed.*, **23,** 17; *I.P.L.*, **33,** 17]
(1938*a*) 'Ein Wort zum Antisemitismus', *Die Zukunft* (Paris), No. 7 (November 25), 2. (92)
[*Trans.:* 'A Comment on Anti-Semitism', *Die Zukunft* (Paris),

No. 7 (November 25); *Standard Ed.*, **23,** 289.]

(1940*a* [1938]) *Abriss der Psychoanalyse*, *G.W.*, **17,** 67. (4–5, 62, 65, 95, 213, 215, 247, 273–4, 280)

[*Trans.: An Outline of Psycho-Analysis*, New York, 1968; London, 1969; *Standard Ed.*, **23,** 141; *I.P.L.*, **35.**]

(1950*a* [1887–1902]) *Aus den Anfängen der Psychoanalyse*, London. Includes 'Entwurf einer Psychologie' (1895). (76, 78, 120, 130)

[*Trans.: The Origins of Psycho-Analysis*, London and New York, 1954. (Partly, including 'A Project for a Scientific Psychology', in *Standard Ed.*, **1,** 175.]

(1960*a*) *Briefe 1873–1939* (ed. E. L. Freud), Frankfurt. (3–4)

[*Trans.: Letters 1873–1939* (ed. E. L. Freud) (trans. T. and J. Stern), New York, 1960; London, 1961.]

(1968*a* [1927-39]) *Sigmund Freud/Arnold Zweig. Briefwechsel* (ed. E. L. Freud), Frankfurt. (3)

[*Trans.: The Letters of Sigmund Freud and Arnold Zweig* (ed. E. L. Freud), London and New York, 1970.]

GARDINER, SIR A. (1927) *Egyptian Grammar*, London. (3rd ed., 1957.) (6)

GRESSMANN, H. (1913) *Mose und seine Zeit: ein Kommentar zu den Mose-Sagen*, Göttingen. (36, 40)

HERLITZ, G. and KIRSCHNER, B. (ed.) (1930) *Jüdisches Lexikon*, **4,** Berlin. (8)

HERODOTUS *History*. (27, 30, 35)

[*Trans.:* Loeb Classical Library (trans. A. D. Godley), London and New York, Vol. I, 1921.]

JONES, E. (1957) *Sigmund Freud: Life and Work*, Vol. 3, London and New York. (Page references are to the English edition.) (3–5, 102)

JOSEPHUS, FLAVIUS, *Jewish Antiquities*. (29, 32)

[*Trans.:* in *Josephus*, **4,** Loeb Classical Library (trans. H. St. J. Thackeray), London and New York, 1930.]

KIRSCHNER, B. and HERLITZ, G. *See* HERLITZ, G. and KIRSCHNER, B.

MANETHO *The History of Egypt*. (105)

[*Trans.:* in *Manetho*, Loeb Classical Library (trans. W. G. Waddell), London and Cambridge Mass., 1940.]

MEYER, E. (1905) 'Die Mosesagen und die Lewiten', *S.B. Akad. Wiss. Berl.* (Phil.-Hist. Kl.), **31,** 640. (15)

(1906) *Die Israeliten und ihre Nachbarstämme*, Halle. (13, 15, 33–7, 45, 49, 61)

RANK, O. (1909) *Der Mythus von der Geburt des Helden*, Leipzig and Vienna. (10–13)

[*Trans.: The Myth of the Birth of the Hero*, New York, 1914.]

SELLIN, E. (1922) *Mose und seine Bedeutung für die israelitisch-jüdische Religionsgeschichte*, Leipzig. (36–7, 47, 51–2, 58, 60–1, 69, 89, 93)

SMITH, LINDON (1956) *Tombs, Temples and Ancient Art*, Oklahoma. (6)

SMITH, W. ROBERTSON (1894) *Lectures on the Religion of the Semites*, new [2nd] ed., London. (1st ed., 1889.) (82–3, 130–2)

SOLOWEITSCHIK, M. (1930) Contribution to *Jüdisches Lexikon* (ed. Herlitz and Kirschner), Berlin, **4** (1), 303. (8)

VOLZ, P. (1907) *Mose: ein Beitrag zur Untersuchung über die Ursprünge der Israelitischen Religion*, Tübingen. (52)

WEIGALL, A. (1922) *The Life and Times of Akhnaton*, new and revised ed., London. (1st ed., 1910.) (24, 25)

YAHUDA, A. S. (1929) *Die Sprache des Pentateuch in ihren Beziehungen zum Ägyptischen*, Berlin. (39, 43)

LIST OF ABBREVIATIONS

G.S.	=Freud, *Gesammelte Schriften* (12 vols.), Vienna, 1924–34
G.W.	=Freud, *Gesammelte Werke*, (18 vols.), London, from 1940
C.P.	=Freud, *Collected Papers* (5 vols.), London, 1924–50
S.E. / *Standard Ed.*	=Freud, *Standard Edition* (24 vols.), London, from 1953
I.P.L.	=International Psycho-Analytical Library, Hogarth Press and Institute of Psycho-Analysis, London, from 1921
Almanach 1938	=*Almanach der Psychoanalyse 1938*, Vienna, Internationaler Psychoanalytischer Verlag, 1937

GENERAL INDEX

This index includes the names of non-technical authors. It also includes the names of technical authors where no reference is made in the text to specific works. For references to specific technical works, the Bibliography should be consulted.—The compilation of the index was undertaken by Mrs. R. S. Partridge.